THOSE SPIRITED
W O M E N
OF THE EARLY WEST

A MINI-HISTORY
by
Phyllis Zauner

ZANEL PUBLICATIONS
P. O. Box 1387
Sonoma, CA 95476

PICTURE CREDITS

Library of Congress: 5, 15, 23; Bancroft Library: 38, 39, 19; Calif. State Library: 21, 31, 32, 40, 41, 42, 44, 52, 53; Western History Coll., U. of Oklahoma: 7, 49, 50, 62, 63; Leslie's Illustrated: 43; Museum of city of New York: 45; Denver Public Library: 25, 63; Western Collection: 24, 15; Calif. Society of Pioneers: 54; Nevada Historical Society: 17, 18, 47, 48, 58, 59, 60; Winchester Mystery House San Jose: 33, 34; Wells-Fargo History Room: 35, 36; Wyoming State Museum: 15; Colorado Historical Society: 15; Oklahoma Historical Society: 62, 63, 61; Calif. Historical Society: 27, 28.

ZANEL publications:

California Gold, Story of the Rush to Riches
Carson City, Capital of Nevada
Lake Tahoe, The Way It Was Then and Now
Sacramento and the California Delta
San Francisco, The Way It Was Then and Now
The Cowboy, An American Legend
Those Legendary Men of the Wild West
Those Spirited Women of the Early West
Virginia City, Its History ... Its Ghosts

Library of Congress Catalog Card Number: 89-50594
ISBN 0-936914-21-1

FRONT COVER
Madame Moustache, Lillie Coit,
Adah Menken, Lola Montez

BACK COVER
Arizona Mary – a "bullwhacker"
on the trail

CONTENTS

Remarkable exploits, previously the domain of men only, were accomplished by these women, who discovered their own talents, resourcefulness — and sometimes outrageous behavior — during their westering experience.

Above all, they were indeed spirited.

— The Author

Westward Ho the Women!

The mass migration from the East to Oregon and California in the 1840s has no precedent in American history, perhaps none in the world. By the hundreds of thousands, men and women pushed on across the continent, forsaking their past lives for land, gold, opportunity, adventure.

The many journals, diaries and letters left by those who made the westward crossing paint a vivid picture of the almost unbelievable human tenacity, ingenuity and raw courage that enabled them to cross 2,000 miles of an alien, hostile land. They battled desert heat and alkali dust, wind-whipped rain that flattened tents, terrifying passes over the Sierra and Cascade mountains, cholera, typhoid fever, and sometimes hostile Indians. They stopped only for birth and death — and sometimes barely that.

Jane Gould Tortilott wrote on her way to California: "We passed a train today where they were digging a grave for a woman that was run over by the cattle and wagons when they stampeded yesterday. She lived 24 hours. She gave birth to a child a short time before she died. The child was buried with her. She leaves a little two-year-old girl and a husband. They say he is nearly crazy with sorrow."

For most of the emigrants, the trip was a spectacular event in their lives, unlike anything they had done before or would ever do again. Impressed by its uniqueness, both men and women were moved to record this once-in-a-lifetime experience in diaries. Men's entries tended to be factual: "Ascended three steep, muddy hills this morning...Made twenty miles today...Paid 1.50 for hay."

Women's accounts were more personal. They observed the people around them, told of events in the lives of other members of their wagon train. They described wonders of nature they had never before seen — spectacular mountain scenery, gorgeous desert sunsets, violent yet thrilling storms, strange new plants and animals.

Not only the awe-inspiring, but the ordinary and mundane found their way into women's musings. Seemingly no natural phenomenon was too small to escape the chronicles. "There were so many beautiful stones along the road," recorded Helen Carpenter, "that we did a great deal of walking just for the pleasure of picking them up to admire for a while. All the colors of the rainbow were represented."

As they traveled, women did the usual chores of preparing meals and caring for children, helped pick up buffalo chips for fuel, sometimes helped drive the oxen teams. They suffered pregnancy and childbirth, and even continued on alone if widowed. According to a study of one group of widows, they never placed their wagons and families under the protection of a male-headed family. All continued on westward, directing the family enterprise alone.

A popular source of fuel was "buffalo chips" – dried dung left by grazing herds.

Some became entrepreneurs, operating a boardinghouse for men far from family who longed for homecooking. In the boom-or-bust frenzy of the gold country, men would pay a high price for bread made by a woman.

Luzena Wilson started a hotel in California by laying two planks together in a tent and setting out a tureen of soup. From the first she was well patronized and later took her husband into partnership,

Not a few women discovered they could make as much as $100 a week doing men's laundry. One woman, widowed on the trail, eked out a living for herself and eight children living out of her covered wagon and ironing shirts on a chair out-of-doors.

A plucky woman they called "Arizona Mary" earned a substantial livelihood driving a 16-yoke ox team, hauling supplies in the Southwest.

Other emigrants became teachers, actresses, nurses, harlots, or missionaries. Florinda Washburn, a milliner by trade and unmarried, who financed her own wagon with a "strapping youth" to drive it, arrived in California gold mining territory in the 1850s and set up a millinery shop. Eventually she became a woman of great wealth.

"Arizona Mary"

Most importantly, these women were all changed in some measure by their westering experience. They began to discover, little by little, the unexplored realms of their own talents.

And above all, they were – indeed! – spirited.

The Settlers

Whatever the perils or pleasures of the trek westward, everyone was grateful to land somewhere and cease their "gypsy" existence.

But the first look at their new homes certainly tested women's fortitude. The lucky ones got crude log cabins without doors or windows, or settled into mining shacks with dirt floors and canvas ceilings. In many parts of the Early West, a log cabin wasn't so easy to come by.

In California during the gold rush, the first abode almost invariably was a tent. The reason was not lack of trees, but lack of manpower. The men were all too busy scratching for gold to take time building.

Keeping food on the table could baffle the most resourceful. "Our fare is very plain, consisting of meat and bread, bread and meat, now and then some rancid butter that was put up in the Land of Goshen and sent on a six-month cruise by Cape Horn, for which we give the sum of $2 a pound.

Meat was usually wild game, preserved by salting and hanging in smokehouse or fireplace. A worse problem was fruits and vegetables. "As we had no jars in which to preserve wild fruit for winter, we cooked it to the consistency of thin paste, put it through a sieve and dried it on large platters before the open fire until it was like leather. These cakes were then hung from the roof beams, taken down when needed, boiled with water and sometimes sweetened."

They learned from the Indians strange edible plants, and considered making bread with acorns until they found that crushed earthworms were used for shortening.

One frontier wife used dandelion roots, roasting them on an iron baking pan until brown, to make "coffee."

To furnish a western home required sufficient ingenuity to use whatever was at hand. One woman, just arrived in California, furnished her canvas abode by converting a wooden box into a trundle bed for her children, upending trunks for closets, and covering some kegs with moss and oil calico for ottoman seats. Mattresses could be made of buffalo hair.

Before kerosene, women melted deer tallow in pans over the fireplace to make candles. Walls were papered with newspapers, and one of the joys of moving into a previously occupied house was "reading the walls."

Still, despite the dirt floors, snakes and centipedes, sagging roofs and leaning walls, women described their first frontier homes with a sense of accomplishment in their ability to cope.

They had a spirit that conquered inconvenience and privation, and brought some ray of sunshine into the most primitive surroundings. One girl recalled how her mother made mirrors by "taking an old black shawl and tacking it smoothly over a board, and placing a pane of some precious window glass in front of it."

Another woman, longing for a change from sagebrush, set up a small willow branch outside her front door and "used artificial flowers that I happened to have to make blooms on the little tree."

Spirit, indeed!

Mary Ballou

Women arriving in Gold Country California frequently found they could make more money taking in laundry or cooking at a boarding-house than their miner husbands who were out there hunkered over a gold pan, up to their ankles in some Sierra stream.

Either way, it was no easy life.

Mary Ballou, who lived at Negro Bar, a mining settlement along the American River, gives a lively account of her day-to-day life in letters she wrote to her son Selden. In parts her account becomes a journal that pours out her emotions and her reactions to a new life in a strange land that was not much like anything she left behind in "the States."

October 20, 1852: My Dear Selden: we are about as usual in health. well I suppose you would like to know what I am doing in this gold region. well I will try to tell you what my work is here in this muddy Place.

All the kitchen that I have is four posts stuck down into the ground and covered over the top with factory cloth no floor but the ground. this is a Boarding House kitchen. There is a floor in the dining room and my sleeping room covered with nothing but cloth. we are at work in a Boarding House.

Oct. 27, 1852: this morning I awoke and it rained in torrents. well I got up and I thought of my House. I went and lookt into my kitchen. the mud and water was over my Shoes I could not go into the kitchen to do any work to day but kept perfectly dry in the Dining. Your Father put on his Boots and done the work in the kitchen. I felt badly to think that I was destined to be in such a place. I wept for a while and then I commenced singing and made up a song as I went along.

Now I will try to tell you what my work is in this Boarding House. well sometimes I am washing and Ironing sometimes I am making mince pie and Apple pie and squash pies. Sometimes frying mince turnovers and Donuts. then again I am making minute puding filled with rasons and Indian Bake pudings and them I am Stuffing a Ham of pork that cost forty cents a pound., sometimes I am making coffee for the French people strong enough for any man to walk on that has faith as Peter had.

sometimes I am feeding my chickens and then again I am scaring the Hogs out of my kitchen and Driving the mules out of my Dining room. you can see that anything can walk into the kitchen and then from kitchen into the Dining room any time day or night if they chooses to do so. sometimes I am up all times a night scaring the Hogs and mules out of the House. last night there a large rat came down pounce down into our bed in the night. sometimes I take my fan and try to fan mysself but I work so hard that my Arms pain me so severely that I kneed some one to fan me so I do not find much comfort anywhere.

I am taking care of Babies and nursing at the rate of Fifty Dollars a week but I could not advise any Lady to come out here and suffer the toil and fatigue that I have suffered for the sake of a little gold neither do I advise any one to come. Clark Simmons wife says if she was safe in the States she would not care if she had not one cent. She came in here last night and said "O dear I am so homesick that I must die." and then again my other associate came in with tears in her eyes and said that she had cried all day. she said if she had as good a home as I had got she would not stay twenty five minutes in California. I told her that she could not pick up her duds in that time. she said she would not stop for duds nor anything else but my own heart was too sad to cheer them much.

now I will tell you a little more about my cooking. sometimes I am cooking rabbits and Birds that are called quails here and I cook squirrels. occasionally I run in and have a chat with Jane and Mrs. Dunphy and I often have a hearty cry. no one but my Maker knows my feelings and then I run into my little cellar which is about four feet square as I have no other place to run that is cool.

———✦———

October 21, 1852. well I have been to church to hear a methodist sermon. his text was let us lay aside every weight and the sin that doth so easily beset us. I was the only Lady that was present and about forty gentlemen. So you see that I go to church when I can.

November 2, 1852. well it has been Lexion day here to day. I have heard of strugling and pulling but never saw such a day as I have witnessed today the Ballot Box was so near to me that I could hear every word that was spoken. the wind Blows verry hard here today. I have three lights Burning and the wind blows so hard that it almost puts my lights out while I am trying to write. if you could but step in and see the inconvenience that I have for writing you could not wonder that I cannot write any better you would wonder that I could write at all. it is quite cold here my fingers are so cold that I can hardly hold my pen. well it is ten oclock at night while I writing the people have been Declaring the votes. I hear them say Hura for the Whigs and sing whig songs now I hear them say that Mormon Island has gone whig. now I hear them say Beals Bar has gone whig now another time cheering. well it is getting late and I must retire soon there is so much noise I do not expect to sleep much to night. there has been a little fighting here to day and one chalenge given but the chalenge was not accepted they got together and settled their trouble.

I will tell you a little of my bad feelings. on the 9 of September there was a little fight took place in the store. I saw them strike each other through the window in the store. one went and got a pistol and started towards the other man.

I never go into the store but your mothers tender heart could not stand that so I ran into the store and Beged and plead with him not to kill him for eight or ten minutes not to take his Life for the sake of his wife and three little children. and then I ran through the Dining room into my sleeping room and Buried my Face in my bed so as not to hear the sound of the pistol and wept Biterly. Oh I thought if I had wings how quick I would fly to the States. that night at the supper table he told the Boarders if it had not been for what that Lady said to him Scheles would have been a dead man. after he got his pashion over he said that

he was glad that he did not kill him so you see that your mother has saved one Human beings Life. you see that I am trying to relieve all the suffering and trying to do all the good that I can.

there I hear the Hogs in my kitchen turning the Pots and kettles upside down so I must drop my pen and run and drive them out. so you see this is the way that I have to write. jump every five minutes for something and then again I washed out about a Dollars worth of gold dust the fourth of July in the cradle so you see that I am doing a little mining in this gold region but I think it harder to rock the cradle to wash out gold than it is to rock the cradle for the Babies in the States.

October 11, 1852: I made a Democrat Flag in the afternoon sewed twenty yards of splendid worsted fringe around it and I made a whig Flag. they are both swinging acrost the road. I had twelve Dollars for making them so you see what I am doing and then again I am scouring candle sticks and washing the floor and making soap. sometimes I am making mattresses and sheets. I have no windows in my room. all the light that I have shines through canvas that covers the House and my eyes are so dim that I can hardly see. I am among the French and Duch and Scoth and Jews and Italions and Sweeds and Chinese and Indians and all manner of tongue and nations but I am treated with due respect by them all.

O my Dear Selden I am so Home sick I will say to you once more to se that Augustus has every thing that he kneeds to make him comfortable and by all means have him Dressed warm this cold winter. I worry a great deal about my Dear children. It seems as though my heart would break when I realize how far I am from my Dear Loved ones this from your affectionate mother. Mary B. Ballou

Virginia Reed

Among the most unfortunate of early westering pioneers was the Reed family, attached to the luckless Donner Party wagon train. It is one of the most tragic stories of the West.

Due to a combination of ineptitude, poor judgment, bickering, and just plain rotten fortune, the entire company found itself stranded in the Sierra mountains for four long wintry months, buffeted by one snowstorm after another, slowly starving to death.

Virginia Reed, who was thirteen at the time, was one of the survivors. She wrote of her experiences on the fateful journey in 1891, when she was in her 60s.

Her father, James Reed, was a well-to-do furniture manufacturer in Springfield, Illinois. The westering bug had bit him because he had ambitions to become an Indian agent for the territory beyond the Rockies.

His wagon, as he started the journey, was a mammoth, two-story affair, well stocked with furnishings and food, drawn by the finest Durham oxen. He even brought along a pony so little Virginia could canter around the prairie.

As they set out on their journey, everyone was there to see them off – even Mrs. Lincoln, whose husband Abe had been an army buddy of Reed's.

"We were all surrounded by loved ones," Virginia recalled in later years, "and there stood all my little schoolmates who had come to kiss me good-bye. My father with tears in his eyes tried to smile as one friend after another grasped his hand in a last farewell. Mama was overcome with grief. At last we were all in the wagons, the drivers cracked their whips, the oxen moved slowly forward and the long journey had begun."

Things went smoothly the first weeks. "Our little home was so comfortable that mama could sit reading and chatting with the three little ones {Virginia's younger siblings} and almost forgot that she was really crossing the plains."

The first of the troubles that were to dog the rest of the journey occurred in Kansas. Virginia sent the bad news back home in a letter she handed to a horseman headed east. "Gramma died, she became speechless the day before she died. We buried her verry decent. We made a nete coffin and buried her under a tree, we had a headstone and had her name cut on it and the date...the young men soded it all over and put Flores on it. We miss her verry much every time we come into the Wagon we look at the bed for her."

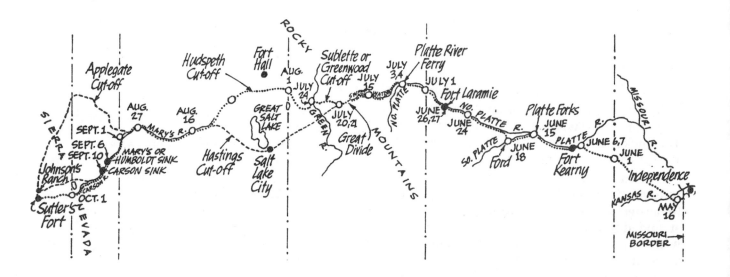

When the wagon train reached Fort Bridger, a disagreement arose as to whether to take the better-known long route. or the Hastings cut-off, 200 miles shorter. The train split into two, and Reed elected to go with the short-route group headed by George Donner. A serious mistake.

The Hastings route turned out to be scarcely a trail, and much time was consumed hacking down underbrush. At the edge of the Great Basin desert they found a tattered note attached to a board: "Two days and two nights of hard driving to reach next grass and water. Hardest going yet."

In actuality, the trip was six days of inhumanly hard going. Wagons sank deep into ash-like sand, the oxen almost collapsed. Everyone was thirsty. Virginia's mother gave her small lumps of sugar moistened with peppermint, and a flattened bullet to chew on, which was supposed to prevent dry throat.

To compound the discomfort, Reed's oxen escaped and were never found, though a precious week was used up in the search.

Then John Reed had an altercation with another man and in anger plunged a knife into him. Although other train members agreed it was self-defense, the victim's death forced them to banish Reed. He was sent out into the desert without a gun.

But as Reed kissed his wife farewell, Virginia slipped him a rifle and ammunition from their wagon, and he headed out alone.

The oxen on Margaret Reed's wagon collapsed from exhaustion, so she had to continue on riding muleback with one child in her lap. Virginia and the other two children shared another mule.

All these delays put the wagon train at the foot of the Sierra mountains far too late in the season. On October 29, the first snows began to fall — unusually early, as luck would have it.

The beleaguered pioneers struggled to push the teams and wagons to reach the summit, but when the snow became waist-deep they had to give up at a place where they found a deserted cabin. Here Margaret Reed and her children settled in with several others, while the rest of the party started building rude shelters for themselves.

They killed the oxen, froze the meat in the snow. But as weeks passed and new snowstorms came upon the tail of the old, the food was almost gone. By January the half-starved immigrants had started boiling the cowhides and eating the glue soup.

It was finally agreed that one group would try to make it out on snowshoes to seek help. Ten days out, the men and children had made little progress and were half-mad with hunger. It was here that the first suggestion was made that they draw lots to see who should die to furnish food for the others. One man refused to be part of the pact, so they decided to slog on until nature took its course and the weakest would die. That eventuality was not long in coming.

Meanwhile, back in the cabin, Mrs. Reed resolved to strike out on foot to seek help. She said good-bye to her younger children and took Virginia and a faithful servant who had come on the trip with them.

It was a ridiculously valiant attempt. Virginia was so weak that on the steeper slopes she had to climb on hands and knees. In this fashion the three actually scaled the pass. They stopped to improvise snowshoes, then went on for another day.

But on the following day Virginia's feet were frost-bitten. There was nothing to do but give up. In some way they managed to get back down over the pass, back to the cabin.

The following day brought yet another snowstorm.

Finally, after many had died and hopelessness had set in, a relief party arrived. James Reed had managed to make his way to Sutter's Fort in Sacramento, and a search party had been organized. On February 19 they arrived with food. Virginia, hearing his voice, leaped forward, trying to run but tripping and falling in the snow from weakness. Her father caught her in his arms.

That was not the end of the Donner Party's trials, for they still had to make the trek out. But they did overcome.

A month later, safe again, Virginia Reed wrote to her cousin in Illinois: "O Mary, I have not wrote you half of the truble we have had but I have Wrote you enuf to let you know that you dont know what truble is but thank the good God we have all got throw and the onely family that did not eat human flesh."

Mrs. Reed, who had so audaciously dared the snowy summits with Virginia, lived another fifteen years, her husband twelve beyond that. Virginia lived a long and happy life in California, married to an Army officer who later became one of the first real estate salesmen in the West. When her husband lost his eyesight, Virginia led him to his office each day and later took over his real estate business — first woman to enter that profession.

A Gallery of Tough Ladies

Women of free spirit and independent mind soon found that in the West they were less constricted by convention. They could live as they pleased.

They rode their horses astride instead of sidesaddle (not too ladylike!) On the ranch, they learned to rope and brand steers and do a "man's work". Some wore buckskins – which some people considered scandalous.

Eager for adventure and challenge, they performed feats of derring-do – simply to prove it could be done by a woman.

On a dare, Eunice Winkless plunged 35 feet on a trained horse, into a pool.

The Miners

A woman in the mines

Mining was backbreaking, discouraging work, and for all who struck it rich, there were thousands who hunkered ankle-deep in cold mountain streams rotating a pan or shovelling a ton of gravel a day into a long tom.

It was work that would have appealed to few women – even if it were an accepted practice of the day.

Indeed, in the early days of 1849 there would have been few women to make a career of it because there were almost no women in camp. According to some statistics, the ratio was two women for a hundred men.

But by late summer 1849, women were starting to arrive in larger numbers. And if none of them actually hankered to toil with a pan or long tom, they did share the same raw life that was the lot of miners, in camps built of muslin and canvas – and also the rousing exuberance that made the Gold Rush the most extraordinary episode in American history.

Every hastily erected canvas camp resounded to the same over-optimistic talk of prospectors, miners, speculators and storekeepers lured by the promise of gold.

Women, too, got caught up in the fever.

Some staked claims in their own name, cheered on the men who worked the claims. Some were wives of men who served the miners. Some married the men who made the fortunes they came for.

Either way, they had a grand adventure they never forgot, living in the midst of high hopes and dashed dreams and the occasional fortunes that came to the lucky almost by accident.

Some women were surprised to find that they, too, were rich beyond their wildest dreams.

Eilley Orrum Bowers

From rags to riches, and back to rags again. All in ten years. That's the tragic story of Nevada's first millionaires, Lemuel "Sandy" Bowers and Allison "Eilley" Orrum Bowers.

Sandy had been a Missouri mule skinner before drifting to Virginia City. People who knew him well described him as "an honest, kindhearted soul, born and reared in the lower ranks of life, and miraculously ignorant."

Eilley came to America as a young girl, from Scotland. She married a Mormon, settled in Nevada; but when Mormons were called back to Salt Lake City, Eilley remained where she was, supporting herself by "doing" for the miners. She cooked and sewed, and sometimes tied up their laundry and took it to the hot springs by a nearby lake. When she grew weary of her labor she would sit on a huge boulder and look over the valley and lake. In her reverie she saw a home – hers – happy children and gay throngs. Later at home, gazing into a crystal ball she had bought years before, she saw the same picture.

One of her boarders who was sick, broke and tired of prospecting, asked Eilley if she would take his ten feet of a claim he had staked out in a ravine in settlement of his board bill. Since it seemed the only way she'd get paid, she accepted. Her claim was next to that of another boarder, Sandy Bowers.

When someone suggested that, with adjoining claims, the owners should be joined too, Eilley's boarder became her husband. The miners of the camp showed their approval by giving the pair a hilarious wedding party.

About this time all hell broke loose in Virginia City, for the famous Comstock Lode had been located. Now this previously insignificant mining camp was on its way to becoming the "richest city on earth."

Soon the Bowers' mines were paying out $18,000 per week. A single candle box of ore produced six hundred dollars. It was so plentiful that visitors to the mines were often given specimens worth a hundred dollars.

In fact, disposing of the rapidly accumulating hoard would have been a burden had it not been for the ambitious Eilley.

Discovery of the fabulous Comstock Lode.

She was determined to make her fondest dreams come true. She started with planning a mansion, to be the finest between St. Louis and San Francisco. And it would be away from the noisy mines and stamp mills — down by Washoe Lake where she had once done the miners' laundry in the hot springs.

To get proper furnishings, such as the Comstock had never seen, a grand trip to Europe was proposed.

At a farewell party, Sandy announced they had "money to throw at the birds," and then they were off on a Grand Tour that lasted a year and a half.

Handsome furniture was made to order in Italy, carpets were specially designed and woven. They ordered dozens of sets of moroccobound books with their name imprinted in gilt (though Sandy was illiterate), selected bedroom furniture heavily carved with grapes. One set of chairs embodied the idea of a throne, high, stiff and formal with a fleur-de-lis carved on each post. Silver bullion was sent from their mine to make a table service.

Eilley had it in mind that they would be received by Queen Victoria, and had clear visions of the cordiality and eagerness with which the nobility would seek these princes of wealth.

To be ready for this royal occasion, Eilley found a couturier in Paris to make her presentation gown — an elaborate model of purple with roses worked in gold thread on the silk background and lace at the throat and wrists.

Alas, Eilley learned that Prince Albert had died, Victoria was in mourning, and in any case didn't receive divorced women.

So with deep disappointment (and carrying a few cuttings of ivy from Westminster Abbey), she returned to Nevada, her home and their mines. They put all the furniture in place and invited all of Virginia City to a big party. Eilley was seated on her throne chair. But the *haute monde* declined.

Her hopes of being presented at Court dashed, Eilley Bowers had her picture taken wearing the dress she had hoped would impress Queen Victoria.

It was a bitter blow. But worse was yet to come. The mine began to peter out. New machinery was bought. The snows piled high all winter. Then the spring thaw filled the mine with mud and slime. Sandy, working all night to save the machinery and the mine, caught cold. It finished Sandy's life.

Sandy's estate was valued at $638,000. Creditors appeared from everywhere. The mill was mortgaged. Sandy had sold so much stock in his mine that he no longer controlled it. His loans to others and his investments were worthless.

Except for the mansion and its expensive furnishings, Eilley was broke.

It wasn't just her mine that was no longer yielding those big returns any more. The real trouble was that the Comstock was not producing. The whole town was in declining circumstances.

Determined not to lose her mansion, she had an ingenious idea. She'd turn it into a high-class resort with swimming pools, greenhouses, fountains with gold fish. To raise the capital for the venture, she proposed to raffle the property.

"Bowers Mansion Entertainment, Tickets $2.50" read the flyers.

The whole transaction was unique. A Chinaman won the rosewood piano, which he couldn't play. Household utensils which she didn't want went to a young girl. Mrs. Bowers drew her own home.

With creditors temporarily satisfied, she was free to turn her home into a resort. A third story with eight bedrooms was added. A dance pavilion was built, space was set aside for croquet grounds.

"Bowers mansion now open for visitors and rural entertainments," she advertised. So great was the appeal that the Virginia & Truckee Railroad built a platform a mile long across the meadow for convenience of its passengers.

Then disaster struck. Eilley's only daughter died. After that she couldn't pick herself up again.

The resort was no longer making money, her creditors lost patience. She lost the home but was given a small cottage on the corner of the estate. Then even that burned to the ground.

Eilley Orrum Bowers was penniless and homeless. She moved in with a friend and made a precarious living with her crystal ball. When that failed, she moved to a basement room in San Francisco to practice her clairvoyance.

Eventually she was placed in a charity home and lived out her life in the company of others who had seen less of romance and tragedy in their lives.

Mrs. Bowers' dream house. Picnickers were invited.

Dame Shirley

Among the best records of day-to-day life in the Gold Rush camps, from a woman's point of view, are the letters of Louise Clappe – Dame Shirley to her friends – who came with her doctor husband to Rich Bar, a dusty mining camp in northern California, in 1851.

In letters to her sister "back in the States" she faithfully recorded the hell-roaring life around her and accurately described everything from mining techniques to the drinking habits of miners. In so doing, she has provided posterity with the human side of the mining frontier, a glimpse of the personal lives of the miners, and a vivid picture of a time and place that was like nothing will ever be again.

Though the horrible was ever present, and perhaps as the wife of a physician she got to see more of it then the usual pioneer, Shirley did not neglect the beautiful and elevating. Her description of the countryside provides an almost photographic view of the mountain country in 1851 and 1852.

Her correspondence lasted a little more than a year; some selected passages hint of the richness of her observations.

September 13, 1851: I wish I could give you some faint idea of the majestic solitudes through which we passed on our way to Rich Bar. The moon was just rising as we started. The air made one think of fairy festivals, of living in the woods always with green-coated people for playmates. It was wonderfully soft and cool, without the least particle of dampness.

September 14, 1851: The hill leading into Rich Bar is five miles long, and as steep as you can imagine. Fancy yourself riding for this distance, along the edge of a frightful precipice, where should your mule make a misstep, you would be dashed hundreds of feet into the awful ravine below. Halfway down we came to a wider level spot, and here the girth of my saddle (which we found to be fastened only by four tacks) gave way and I fell over the side of the mule. I was not hurt, but had the accident happened at any other part of the hill I must have been dashed into the dim valleys beneath.

September 20, 1851: Today I visited the "doctor's office," and the shock to my optic nerves was so great I laughed till I cried. There was, of course, no floor; a rude table in one corner held the medical library, consisting of half a dozen volumes. The shelves, which looked like sticks snatched from the wood pile contained quite a respectable array of medicines.

September 15, 1851: We are safely ensconced under the magnificent roof of the "Empire," which is one of the shanties on the Bar that claims to be a hotel. Indeed, California might be called the Hotel State, so completely is she inundated with boardinghouses and taverns. It is the only two-story building in town, built of planks of the roughest possible description. The roof, of course, is covered with canvas, which also forms the entire front of the house, on which is painted in immense capitals, "THE EMPIRE!" There are also two or three glass windows, an unknown luxury in all the other dwellings.

April 10, 1852: The other day a hole caved in, burying up to the neck two unfortunates who were in it at the time. Luckily they were but slightly injured.

The doctor is at present attending a man at the junction who was stabbed very severely in the back during a drunken frolic. The people have not taken the slightest notice of this affair, although for some days the life of the wounded man was despaired of. The perpetrating of the deed had not the slightest provocation from his unfortunate victim.

May 1, 1852: Our countrymen are among the most discontented of mortals. They are always longing for "big strikes." If a "claim" is paying them a steady income by which they could lay up more in a month than they could accumulate in a year at home, they are still dissatisfied, and will wander off in search of better diggings.

July 5, 1852: A few evenings ago a Spaniard was stabbed by an American. It seems that the presumptuous foreigner had the impertinence to ask very humbly that most noble representative of the stars and stripes if the latter would pay him a few dollars owed him for some time. His high mightiness, the Yankee, was not going to put up with any such impertinence, and the poor Spaniard received, for answer, several inches of cold steel in his breast, which inflicted a very dangerous wound. Nothing was done, and very little was said about the atrocious affair.

October 22. 1852: I ought to say a word about the dances which we have in the bar room, a place so low that a very tall man could not have stood upright in it. One side was fitted up as a store, and another with bunks for lodgers. These bunks were elegantly draperied with red calico, through which we caught dim glimpses of blue blankets. On ball nights the bar is very quiet and respectable. To be sure, there is some danger of being swept away in a flood of tobacco juice; but luckily the floor is uneven, and it lays around in puddles, which with care one can avoid, merely running the minor risk of falling prostrate upon the wet boards in the midst of a gallopade.

November 21, 1852: In many places on the mountains the snow is already five feet in depth. Since so many people are leaving for the valley, it is hoped the path will be kept open, so I can make the journey out of here with comparative ease on a horse.

My heart is heavy at the thought of departing forever from this place. I *like* this wild and barbarous life; I leave it with regret. The solemn fir trees, the watching hills, and the calmly beautiful river, seem to gaze sorrowfully at me, as I stand in the moonlighted midnight, to bid them farewell.

Yes, Molly, smile if you will at my folly; but I go from the mountains with a deep heart sorrow. I look kindly at this existence, which to you seems so sordid and mean. Here, at least, I have been contented.

Baby Doe Tabor

Colorado's silver mines produced millionaires by the score, but none with the extravagances of lifestyle shared by H.A.W. Tabor and his dazzling second wife, "Baby Doe."

Tabor arrived on the silver scene with his first wife Augusta in 1859 at the height of the get-rich fever. They opened a small store in Oro City, a town so remote that when the miners saw Augusta they were so glad to have a woman around they built her a cabin. Horace was the town postmaster, Augusta ran the store. He dreamed of great riches; she just hoped for a pump outside her front door so she wouldn't have to haul water from the creek.

Horace's dream came true when a couple of luckless prospectors he had staked to $17 worth of food, scratched a rock that proved to be veined with silver. Horace owned one-third of it — $500,000 worth.

It was the start of a great fortune, most of it acquired by luck rather than skill. He bought the Matchless Mine, which yielded a fortune each and every month. Everything he touched seemed to turn to money.

He could hardly spend it fast enough.

But Augusta didn't share his lavish tastes. When Horace finally persuaded her to move to the Denver mansion he had built, she insisted on living in the servants' quarters so she could be near the kitchen. She kept a tethered milk cow in the yard.

In this house, Horace and Augusta lived humbly and became millionaires.

But old Horace was quite a sport. While Augusta was home in the kitchen, he spent his time playing poker in the company of a gorgeous blond, Elizabeth Doe, a young divorcee just arrived from Central City.

They became inseparable, and when Tabor outgrew Leadville he put Baby Doe up in a hotel suite at the Hotel Windsor, which he had just bought.

It was a fitting background for Baby Doe's style. The Windsor was the wonder of Colorado. With 300 rooms, all with fireplaces, it also featured a ballroom floor slung on cables to provide built-in bounce. For cleanliness addicts there were 60 bathtubs, a swimming pool and steam baths.

The WINDSOR

The Tabor theatre in Denver.

He next presented Denver with a splendiferous opera house. But on opening night, Tabor's box was empty. He was estranged from the wife who had sustained him through 26 hardscrabble years, and he was off living the good life with Baby Doe, who understood him better.

Tabor eventually induced Augusta to divorce him, and when he went off to Washington D.C. to fill out the last 30 days of a Senator's seat, it was Baby Doe who went with him.

After a sumptuous wedding ceremony in Washington, he and Baby Doe returned to Denver and settled into a suite at the Windsor, where Tabor had one room permanently reserved for his poker sessions. Occasionally he amused his bride by flinging handfuls of silver dollars from the balcony to the scrambling crowds below.

Nothing was too much for Baby Doe. Horace spent money on her as though it would have no end. He showered her with exquisite jewelry, including a $90,000 diamond necklace.

She knew how to spend money too. She went through $300,000 a month just for living expenses.

Baby Doe longed for respectable domesticity and talked Horace into buying her a mansion. She filled the lawns with cast-iron animals and a few alabaster nudes that shocked the ultra-proper.

Silver kings, politicians, sporting men of all sorts, actors and concert artists attended Baby Doe's parties, but she never quite made the grade with Denver high society. Denver had reached the stage of putting on airs, and to the high-nosed matrons of the city, Baby Doe wasn't "one of us."

Meanwhile, Tabor's investments were all going sour. And in spite of his lobbying, the United States went off the silver standard. Mines closed down all over Colorado.

Over a period of fourteen years, the Tabors had spent $12 million in cash. At that, he had not bothered to pay many of his bills. Not that he was ever pressed for payment — he was, after all, a multi-millionaire.

But the day of reckoning finally came. Baby Doe had to move out of her mansion, the furniture and art treasures were auctioned off to honor his unpaid bills and gambling debts. All that was left were Baby Doe's jewels and the closed and worthless Matchless mine.

The next few years were a nightmare. Baby Doe, so well adjusted to lavish living, now lived in grubby rooms in cheap boardinghouses. Horace worked as a laborer in Leadville for $3 a day. Baby Doe's jewels were sold or pawned as needed to buy food and pay the rent.

Finally Horace's former political pals got him appointed Denver postmaster, a job that paid $3,500 a year – scarcely enough to pay his bar bills in other times.

But if Baby Doe couldn't live in her former high style, at least they ate regularly.

They had fifteen months of relative security, then Tabor was stricken and died of acute appendicitis.

His last words to Baby Doe set the pattern for the balance of her life: "Never let the Matchless go if I die, Baby. It will make millions again once silver comes back."

For the next twelve years Baby Doe eked out a skimpy living in Denver and Leadville, selling a piece of jewelry once in a while to keep herself going. Finally she moved into the cold, dark toolhouse cabin of the Matchless to save rent. There she lived out her life in abject poverty, never giving up hope that silver would come back, as Horace had prophesied on his deathbed.

In the little wooden cabin at the mouth of the Matchless mine, the once-fabulous Baby Doe eked out a miserable existence, her daughters gone – one to marry and live elsewhere, and one to die under dubious conditions in a shabby roominghouse in Chicago. In palmier days, the first-born, Lillie, had been christened in a gown that cost $15,000.

From time to time, Baby Doe walked down to Leadville to buy leftover scraps for food, her feet wrapped in gunny-sacks in winter. And here, by the mine Horace had promised would again make her rich, her frozen body was found.

On March 8, 1935, her frozen body was found in her cabin, but the exact date of her death is unknown.

Augusta, meanwhile, had prospered and moved to California. She invested her money wisely, and at her death left her estate of $1.5 million to her son.

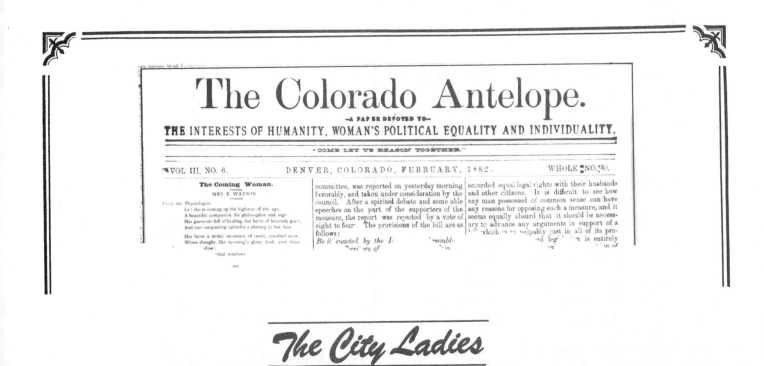

The Colorado Antelope.

—A PAPER DEVOTED TO—

THE INTERESTS OF HUMANITY, WOMAN'S POLITICAL EQUALITY AND INDIVIDUALITY.

"COME LET US REASON TOGETHER."

VOL III, NO. 6.   DENVER, COLORADO, FEBRUARY, 1882.   WHOLE NO. 30.

The Coming Woman.

MRS. E. WATSON

From the Physiologist.

Lo! she is coming up the highway of the age,
A beautiful companion for philosopher and sage;
Her garments full of healing, her heart of heavenly grace,
And love-surpassing splendor a shining in her face.

Her brow a mimic mountain of sweet, unsullied snow,
Where thought, like morning's glory doth ever shine
     slow;

committee, was reported on yesterday morning favorably, and taken under consideration by the council. After a spirited debate and some able speeches on the part of the supporters of the measure, the report was rejected by a vote of eight to four. The provisions of the bill are as follows:

Be it enacted by the Legislative Assembly of the Territory of ...

accorded equal legal rights with their husbands and other citizens. It is difficult to see how any man possessed of common sense can have any reasons for opposing such a measure, and it seems equally absurd that it should be necessary to advance any arguments in support of a bill which is so palpably just in all of its provisions...

The City Ladies

The lure of precious metals brought not only the pick-and-shovel brigade, but also entertainers, artists, speculators and the well-to-do. Civilized cities grew where once there had been nothing but open space.

San Francisco, blessed with an agreeable site on the bay and the mining district nearby, early and easily achieved standards of culture and cosmopolitan ways.

Even in its formative years, it was taking on the tone that was to make it distinctive ever after. Mary Jane Megquier, the harried operator of a large boarding house (whose account follows), found agreeable diversion in mingling with the actors and artists who crowded the theaters and concert halls.

By the 1860s, San Francisco was called "the gayest, lightest-hearted, most pleasure-loving city of the western continent."

Much the same situation prevailed in Denver when the new silver bonanza converted shopkeepers, miners, and shoestring bankers into millionaires.

Newly rich mining kings who had previously survived on a diet of beans now washed down their superbly prepared trout and wild fowl with fine wines imported from France.

The increasingly luxurious tastes of Denver's increasingly well-heeled citizens were reflected in handsome hotels like the Windsor, built largely with the funds of H.A.W. Tabor, onetime New England stonecutter who stumbled into unheard-of wealth. Wonderful theaters featured plays and variety shows. An elegant opera house was well attended.

These were flamboyant, free-wheeling days — times that produced the dashing Bloomer girls, crusaders for women's suffrage, a woman candidate for president, and a bevy of high-spirited individualists who pulled out all the stops to be recognized.

They produced some uncommon, outlandish characters of a sort that has long since disappeared from the social scene.

Mary Jane Megquier

Until 1848, Dr. Thomas Megquier and his wife Mary Jane were living in New England, where he practiced medicine with indifferent success. A family friend then serving as U. S. Consul in the Sandwich Islands (Hawaii) persuaded him to move there and open a medical office in connection with the consulate.

The Megquiers were making plans to do so when the gold excitement in California induced him to change his destination to San Francisco. At first he expected to go alone, but the probable need for his wife's help led to a change of plan.

The Megquiers left their children in the care of a relative, and undertook the California venture together, going by way of Panama. It is believed that Mary Jane was the first American woman to cross the Isthmus. He was one of the first American physicians to open an office in San Francisco.

Things went well for the doctor from the start in the booming financial climate of California.

In time, Mary Jane opened a boarding house which added a considerable revenue to the substantial income derived from the doctor's practice.

Her letters home, written to her children and others, contain little of the melodrama of the Gold Rush days, but much of the commonplace stuff of people's daily life – in particular the reactions of ordinary Americans from a small-town background transplanted to a tumultuous, swashbuckling, unconventional society.

San Francisco, 1850

September 19, 1849: Here we are in the city of dust. There are two establishments here that coin gold, I have seen none coined for less than $5. Gambling is carried on in the largest scale, from five to twenty-five thousand is not infrequently won and lost in the turning of a card.

November 11, 1849: The mines are yielding about the same as when first discovered but it is mighty hard work to get it. Many go there who never done a day's work in their life, dig for a day without success, and return in disgust saying it is all a humbug. Now it is beginning to rain which makes the streets nearly impassable, the mud is a foot deep. The Dr often makes fifty dollars a day in his practice, then we have boarders to pay our house rent.

April 19, 1850: I have a fine view of the bay (over all other buildings) which is filled with shipping from all parts of the world, and makes the cook room delightful. I can stand by the stove and watch the porridge and take a look at the big ships as they are rolling lazily in the water.

May 13, 1850: Your Father is quite unwell and very low spirited, if he does not improve soon I shall not return to you until fall. Yesterday we went aboard the ship of Capt. Mann, who has a right nice wife. She attended a party with us. Her husband don't dance and mine was not able to attend but we cut around right smart, perhaps you'll envy your Mother but you need not, for I have to work mighty hard, and such a horrible climate, the house is filled with dust all the time, a family of twenty to cook for. I have been washing in two spoonfuls of water now for two days, and many other conveniences which make it mighty pleasant.

June 16, 1850: I am now without help again which makes me quite homesick. The husband of the woman I had came back from the mines and I was obliged to give her up. There has been another fire and we have again been obliged to pack up our duds, but as good luck would have it the fire was subdued before it reached us. I am heartily sick of picking up and getting ready to move. I hope my next packing will be for the states. The fire has burned the house we had our parties in.

January 19, 1851: We have the Prefect living with us, which in Cal. is some pumpkins being the highest office in the city, a little fussy but remarkable polite to the ladies.

July 12, 1851: We have a maiden lady boarding here, last Saturday eve I think she had a bite; but whether she will succeed in pulling him in remains to be told. It would be such a nice thing to have a wedding here. Mrs. Davis and myself took a walk to happy valley where we saw some beautiful pansies and foxglove of every color. We strayed into a Chinese hotel where were hundreds of Chinese with their luggage which consisted mostly of baskets with covers.

Capt. Mann arrived today with a cargo of Chile women.

May 31, 1852: Lola Montez is making quite a stir here now but many say that her playing is of the character that it is not proper for respectable ladies to attend but I do want to see her very much. Mr. Clark said in dancing the spider dance she performs the antics of one with a tarantula upon her person and some thought she was obliged to look rather higher for it than was proper in so public a place.

June 15, 1853: Duelling is now the order of the day, there has been three with one party shot, died, a fine young man of 22 and it seems to have cooled their blood considerably.

After two years in San Francisco, the Megquiers returned to Maine for a visit, but a month later they returned to "the city of dust and eternal wind," as her letters described it. A few months later, Mary Jane opened another boarding house and drove herself night and day to keep it in successful operation.

Sometime in 1854 the doctor's health became dangerously impaired and the Megquiers returned to Maine. Apparently some serious marital difficulty developed and Mrs. Megquier sailed for Nicaragua without her husband, en route again to California.

Late in October she reached what had finally become for her "the good city of San Francisco," from which she had no desire to return. Settling her husband's business affairs and running a boarding house occupied most of her time, but she found some leisure for theaters, concerts, and a pleasant social life with intimate friends.

November 29, 1853: The very air I breathe seems so very free that I have not the least desire to return. Mr. Johnson who used to board with us and came on the steamer with me told me he would furnish me with funds if I would take a house he found on the same street I have ever lived on. So I took the house hoping to get a boarder or two, enough to support myself. I borrowed one hundred which you know goes but little ways, but I hope to have a boarder to fill the vacant room which will just pay for the bread I eat and rent. But I assure you I have never for a moment regretted that I left Winthrop, that beautiful house has no charms for me at present and should I know I would never visit it again, it would give me no sorrow if I should have the trials I have endured there.

Dr. Megquier died in Winthrop in 1855. Mary Jane remained in California for at least another year and perhaps much longer.

Mammy Pleasant

Angel or Arch Fiend in the "House of Mystery?" — so read the headline in a Sunday edition of the San Francisco *Call*. Stories about Mary Ann Pleasant abounded in the late 19th century — and most of them had some element of truth.

Was she a saint or a sinner?

This is the long unanswered question about the mysterious figure who became known as "Mammy" Pleasant, a woman who for almost half a century wielded a strange and sinister influence on some of San Francisco's leading citizens. She possessed a fortune at a time when most black women made less than fifteen dollars a month.

Mary Ann Pleasant was a Georgia slave whose quick intelligence and lively tongue had caught her owner's attention. He sent her to Boston to be educated, but instead of returning to the plantation, she met and married a wealthy black Bostonian. After his death, - Mary Ann emigrated to San Francisco with fifty thousand dollars in capital and a plan to set up a boarding house of elegance and distinction.

As things turned out, she was so successful that she eventually owned several of them.

To her swank "boarding houses for bachelors," as they were called, came each night in the 1850s and 1860s, men of wealth and position who were without homes or ties in the still new frontier city, to enjoy the excellence of her table and to meet girls of beauty and class.

There was also her "Geneva Cottage," discreetly isolated in the country, where a select few of her clients were taken for nights of wild revelry with her "proteges."

She attracted a fashionable clientele — people like Senator William Sharon and financier

William Ralston, politician David Broderick, and Judge David S. Terry.

They made Mrs. Pleasant a wealthy woman. She knew all the private indiscretions and quirks of the city's leading males, and could have rattled a lot of bones if she wanted to. She never did.

She was known to be a fabulous cook. Her recipes were almost as big a drawing card as her girls. And while she was serving as hostess over tables laden with her fabled cuisine and homemade brandies, she was also listening to the financial inside information that would next day take her to her stock broker for yet another successful investment.

So completely did these financiers trust Mrs. Pleasant that she soon took as much part in these conversations as if she too were a promoter. The men asked her opinions on various stock manipulations or thanked her for some previous tip. One evening one of them remarked that the best way to get rich in San Francisco was to "know Mammy" – a sobriquet that stuck.

However, many people feared Mammy. It was said that she practiced voodoo and had the evil eye — a myth that might have been magnified by the strange fact that she had one brown eye and one blue.

The real force behind all Mrs. Pleasant's carefully laid plans was her driving ambition to become a bona fide member of San Francisco society – not as a second-rate black woman, but as an accepted equal.

Through Mammy's manipulations, many of her girls – always dressed and coiffed in high fashion and wearing genuine jewels – made brilliant marriages or entered into profitable alliances.

One of her most frequent guests was Thomas Bell, a wealthy banker said to be the power behind William Ralston, head of the Bank of California. Through Mammy's efforts he became enamored of a bubble-headed beauty named Teresa Clingan, who Mammy had groomed for a life of high-style elegance.

In time, Bell and Teresa were living together in a house of Mammy's design – a three-story mansard home with a mirror-lined ballroom and a grand central court.

Then Mammy moved in with them.

Thomas Bell

Teresa Clingan

Soon she was running every aspect of Bell's life. When his friends came to call she refused to admit them, saying he was either "out" or "did not care to see anyone." The house, shrouded in vines and shuttered windows, presented a forbidding exterior, notorious for its secrets. It became known, as far abroad as London and Paris, as the "House of Mystery." It was rumored that the house did not even belong to Thomas Bell, but to Mrs. Pleasant.

Teresa, too, was allowed few visitors. Now a virtual prisoner she wrote in her diary of being "Mary Ann's slave."

Then one day Bell and Teresa had a violent quarrel. Instead of separating, the couple agreed to divide the house. Bell would live in one half, Teresa in the other, and Mammy would act as go-between.

This weird *menage a trois* lasted for twenty years. When in later life Bell announced that he wanted children, word was sent through Mammy, and an arrangement made whereby Teresa would receive $50,000 for every child she bore him. It is said that the child wasn't Bell's at all, but a foundling that Mammy smuggled into the house, but nobody ever managed to prove that.

Now the story takes on a Gothic flavor. As Bell grew older and more senile, his faculties began to deteriorate. He continually turned to Mammy for advice on financial matters, almost totally in her power.

Mammy did everything. She ruled with an iron hand. Neighbors could see her marching off to market each day, a striking figure in her black dress and wide-brimmed hat. What went on inside the big mansion no one knew.

One night Bell fell from the third-floor balcony into the court. Hours later he was dead. Some said he'd been pushed, but again there was no real proof. Mammy continued living in the house until her death.

A strange woman, a strange tale.

But what is often left out is the fact that Mammy was also one of the earliest civil rights heroines.

In the years before the Civil War, Mammy Pleasant went South and secretly helped thousands of blacks escape to Canada. She became known among anti-slavery forces as "the western terminus" of the Underground Railroad.

Driven by her rambunctious nature, Mary Ann Pleasant authored one of the first sparks of black rebellion in San Francisco. The incident occurred as she and two friends decided to take a street car home after shopping. Because of their dark skin, Mrs. Pleasant and one friend were turned away while the other lighter-skinned woman was allowed to ride.

Mrs. Pleasant strode off to find an attorney and returned to file suit against the street-car company. She managed to collect minimal damages in this, one of the first discrimination cases ever brought by a woman.

There's a house in San Jose, California that is as out-of-the-ordinary as the woman who began building it more than a century ago.

Sarah was the belle of New Haven, Connecticut when she married William Winchester, son of the inventor of the repeating rifle – the "Gun That Won the West."

The Winchester rifle, it is said, "killed more game, more Indians and more U. S. soldiers than any other weapon in the nation's history."

Tragedy struck the Winchesters early when they lost a month-old baby girl. Sarah never completely recovered from the baby's death – which may have had some influence on her later eccentricities.

Added to the loss of the child was the death of her husband fifteen years later. She was devastated.

Although the young widow was left roughly $20 million plus enough Winchester Company stock to bring in a thousand dollars a day (at a time when a dollar was really a dollar and there was no income tax), nothing could compensate for her grief.

Searching for the key to happiness, Sarah visited a medium who suggested that her double tragedy was caused by the angry ghosts of Civil War soldiers, Indians and others killed by Winchester weapons. Worse, it was hinted that Sarah might be next to go.

There was a way out. She could start building a house and never stop. As long as there was the sound of hammering, the ghosts would be repelled.

So Sarah left her home in New England, crossed the continent to the sunshine of California, and for almost four decades employed dozens of carpenters and other craftsmen who worked (some say around the clock) building, tearing down, rebuilding, adding to, altering and polishing a sprawling complex that at one time had as many as 750 rooms (of which 160 remain).

Among the many wacky features still visible in the Winchester mansion:

• A staircase that rises to the ceiling, then stops cold.

• A "Seance" room with an odd window that looks down on one of six kitchens.

• A staircase that zig-zags seven times through more than 100 linear feet of tiny, two-inch steps to rise just one story.

• An entryway that allows Winchester carriages to be driven directly into the house for total privacy.

• A staircase of seven steps leading down, followed immediately by eleven steps leading straight up.

• A window that faces the wall of an elevator shaft.

• A tall cupboard an inch and a half deep.

Was Sarah Winchester befuddled, or has the passage of time turned her eccentricities into legend?

The answer is lost in the mists of antiquity. But one certainty remains: Sarah was inventive beyond her time. Some of her innovations presaged modern building techniques:

• A window catch patterend after the Winchester rifle trigger and trip-hammer.

• Cornerplates on stairways to prevent dust pockets.

• An inside crank to open and close outside shutters.

• Her 47 fireplaces had the first hinged iron drops for ashes.

• Tubs in her immense laundry had moulded-in washboards.

A century later, the mystery of tiny, 4'10" Sarah Winchester remains unsolved.

Did the spirits move her?

Did she sit in her Seance room and receive instructions from those long gone?

Have the spirits been mollified now that Sarah is gone?

Today no one lives in the eerie, sprawling mansion, but it is open for all to see the eccentricities created by its eccentric owner.

But the intriguing question remains: WHY DID SHE DO IT?

The only known photo of Sarah Winchester, taken by a gardener hiding in the bushes and held secretly. Mrs. Winchester destroyed all pictures of herself.

Lillie Coit

Perpetual darling of San Francisco's gilded age was Lillie Hitchcock Coit. At a time when the conduct of females was circumscribed by austere convention, Lillie was a dedicated eccentric.

In back rooms she played poker, drank bourbon and smoked black cigars. She once staged a middleweight boxing match in her hotel room. Another time she managed to slip into the all-male Bohemian Club by disguising herself as a gentleman.

Lillie came west with her wealthy Kentucky parents in 1851 at the age of seven and, following the tragic fire that killed two of her playmates, became entranced — one might say obsessed — with firemen.

She became the regular mascot of Knickerbocker Fire Company No. 5, following its members to all conflagrations, cheering them on to deeds of daring and even extinguishing fires. She saluted their night calls by keeping a light burning in her window until the horses hauled the engine back to the firehouse.

She wore a gold pin with a miniature helmet, and sewed the number 5 into her underwear in needlepoint. Each year on the Company's birthday, Lillie would appear at the banquet dresssed in a red fireman's shirt atop a black silk dress. Around her waist was a huge-buckled firemen's belt, and she carried her shiny black fire helmet in one hand.

Often she rode the engine in parades, and she sometimes treated the tired and dirty men to supper after a difficult fight with a blaze.

She took to signing her name "Lillie Hitchcock 5."

Later, when Lillie thwarted her mother's social ambitions by falling in love with the "unsuitable" Howard Coit, she was swept off to Paris, where her novel personality made her a favorite at the court of Napoleon III. There, between gala social events, she acted as courier for the American Confederacy.

Back home in San Francisco, she flaunted every social convention to win back the attentions of Howard Coit, then eloped with him. She continued her eccentricities, and once shaved her head to annoy her husband, alternating wearing a red, a black, and a blond wig.

For a while, the Coits settled in a country house in Calistoga in California's wine region, where one summer Lillie met and befriended Robert Louis Stevenson, who was living with his bride in a miner's cabin in nearby Silverado.

In an age when ladies and liquor were never mentioned in the same breath, she chose to pose with a bottle in her hand.

Occasionally, after a night on the town, dressed in men's clothes, Lillie needed a little help getting home.

She had only a year left in San Francisco before she died. She was cremated wearing her beloved gold pin of Engine Company Number Five.

She left one-third of her estate to the city of San Francisco, part of which was used to build a tower – Coit Tower – which, it is said, resembles a fire hose nozzle.

But respectability never suited Lillie, and the marriage to Coit was not a happy one. When he died suddenly, she went back to her old ways. She moved into a suite at the Palace Hotel.

Here, in her hotel sitting room, came one of her old acquaintances from days when she championed the Confederacy, and he shot one of her visiting friends. He was hauled off to jail, but Lillie was terrified he'd come back and finish her off, too.

She fled San Francisco and spent the next twenty years wandering the world, swearing she would not return until the man was dead.

The Entertainers

Almost with the first prospectors in the West, arrived the first actors.

The early theaters were installed by saloon keepers who were willing to try anything that would draw a crowd. Players imported to entertain the patrons were frequently as rough-hewn as the surroundings. But while these rough halls were played by many entertainers barely worthy of the name, they also attracted some professionals of real talent.

First theater in California was the Eagle in Sacramento – gateway to the gold fields – built in 1849. Entrance to the theater was through the Round Tent Saloon next door, where patrons purchased their tickets, generally pouring out a quantity of gold valued by the ticket seller at $12 an ounce. To reach the upstairs seats, theater-goers had to climb a ladder on the outside. To protect the modesty of the ladies, a piece of canvas was primly tacked to the underside of the ladder.

First member of the cast to be recruited was John Bowman Atwater, a roving actor who arrived in the city broke and barefoot. Most of the remaining troupe came from a disbanded battalion of soldiers passing through town.

San Francisco's first theater, like the Eagle, occupied a second story above a saloon. Opening night was slightly marred by the building sinking several inches into the ground under the weight of the playgoers.

In the gold rush town of Mokelumne Hill a theater with raised stage and candles for footlights was installed in the back part of a saloon. For a performance of Richard III some playful miners smuggled in a jackass and hid it under the stage. When Richard exclaimed, "My kingdom for a horse!" someone kicked the animal vigorously so it responded with a bray.

Tom Maguire, a dapper but uneducated Irishman who gave San Francisco its most popular theater, also brought culture to Virginia City, Nevada.

Maguire's Opera House in Virginia City was the forerunner of Piper's Opera House, which in its later version was a marvel of magnificence, with a spring-supported floor, carpeted aisles, elegant trappings, boxes for the nabobs, a sloped stage (to compensate for the level theater floor), and a guaranteed full house composed of patrons of every persuasion. Some of the luminaries who attended performances were Presidents Grant, Polk and Harrison.

Traveling players were the backbone of theater in the West, and they went everywhere.

One troupe playing `Uncle Tom's Cabin. in rowdy Tombstone, Arizona, had an unnerving experience when Eliza was crossing an imaginary frozen river with a well-trained bloodhound at her heels. A cowboy in the audience rose to her rescue and shot the dog down.

Lola Montez

The 1849 Gold Rush brought adventurers, misfits and romantics of every description to California – but none so electrifying as Lola Montez, fiery actress, outrageous dancer, and general hell-raiser.

Legends of her delicious sinfulness and international scandal have spun down through the years until they are a part of the fabric of western history.

In Europe she had been feted as a raven-haired beauty with eyes like burning coals. Impartial observers who saw her arrive in California thought she may have been a bit past her prime; still her spirited performances injected an element of glamour into the often tawdry routine of the mining camps, and men flocked to see a real European countess on the stage.

Lola started life modestly enough. Born in Ireland in 1818 to a British army officer and his part-Spanish wife, she was christened Eliza Gilbert. But it was her destiny to become the sensation of Europe, both for her theatrical performances and her freewheeling personal life. Her unbounded ambition and extravagant tastes led her through profitable relationships with many of Europe's aristocratic and political elite.

Enamored of Franz Liszt, desired at various times by Victor Hugo, Alexander Dumas and Czar Nicholas I, she became for two years the pampered mistress of Ludwig I, aging king of Bavaria. He adored her, consulted her on political matters, and conferred on her the title of Countess of Landsfeldt, with an annual income of $100,000.

But the tempestuous Countess had a talent for stirring up trouble, and when her escapades incensed King Ludwig's cabinet beyond endurance, the crafty and beautiful young Irish girl was booted off the continent for good.

And so in 1851 Lola embarked on a tour of America's stages, eventually making her way to San Francisco where she made a striking figure strolling the streets with two greyhounds on a leash and an enormous parrot on her shoulder. At theaters her famous beauty and notoriety packed the audiences, though her mediocre acting abilities failed to impress even the woman-hungry miners.

Short on talent perhaps, but long on chutzpah, she inserted a brief biographical note in her program: "I am Lola Montez. I am now 27 years old. I was born in the year 1830 in Seville, the capital of Andalusia, land of serenades and balconies, of troubadors and romances – the fatherland of Miquel Cervantes, of Las Casas, of the Roman Emperors Trajan and Theodosius." None of it was true. Lola had acquired a new identity.

She also acquired a husband, San Francisco newspaperman Patrick Hull. They spent an idyllic six-week honeymoon camping along California's rivers – the Sacramento, Feather and American – from which Lola emerged suntanned and strong. Hull was exhausted.

The tour de force of Lola's repertoire was her famous "Spider Dance," an outrageous performance in which she whirled, stamped, wriggled and writhed to elude tarantulas in her petticoats. The spiders, fashioned of cork, whalebone and rubber, were designed so they seemed to jump at her from the depths of her costume. In portraying her part, Lola shook them out in risque style.

Although contemporary reviews of the Spider Dance fail to elucidate just how all this was done, an August 1856 letter to the editor of the San Francisco Evening Bulletin gives some idea of the experience.

Dear Editor: I had heard that the Spider Dance was supposed to represent a girl that commences dancing and finds a spider on her clothes and jumps about to shake it off. I guess she must see this spider on the ceiling...she kicked up and kicked down in all directions, first this leg and then the other, and her petticoats was precious short.

Then she was going to stoop down and take a rest, when she saw the spider dropping right on to her and she got excited like and worked her body round and round and squirmed like a snake, then she jumped up and kicked so high. A man upstairs hollered Hey! Hey! and people all over commenced hollering. If the Countess wasn't crazy, I don't know what on earth was the matter. She seemed to get so excited like, that she forgot there were any men around, she didn't even see the fiddlers right under her nose. She was going on like mad, lifting her petticoats right up and shaking them!

The people hollering at her seemed to excite her more and more, and the people upstairs and down were all hooping now just like Indians. I puts my hat on and jumped over the back of the seat and made a break for the door and didn't feel safe until I was on the other side of the street. Mr. Editor, I saw more than I wanted to, and I ain't used to it.

To sustain her lavish standard of living, Lola continued to perform on stage. But later that year, visiting the Eureka Mines where she held stock, Lola was inspired to abandon her career and retire to a modest house in the gold country to write her memoirs.

In 1854 Lola Montez, the gifted, the beautiful, the wayward, moved to Grass Valley and made it the scene of her eccentricities for two years. She arrived in town with her husband, some monkeys, a pet bear, and a trunk full of low-cut velvet gowns.

Once, as the mistress of the Bavarian king, she had dazzled Europe. She didn't dazzle Grass Valley.

"She still retained a slender, graceful figure," reported one of Lola's neighbors. "She had heavy black hair and the most brilliant, flashing eyes I have ever beheld. But ordinarily she was such a slattern that to me she was frankly disgusting. When attired in a low-necked gown as was her usual custom, even her liberal use of powder failed to conceal the fact that she stood much in need of a good application of soap."

One day Lola found her pet bear dead and suspected her husband of the crime. They had a terrible row and she sent him packing.

Many were her escapades while in Grass Valley, but the most prominent was the attempt to cowhide the editor of the local newspaper, the *Telegraph*.

Between the two there was considerable ill feeling, and when editor Shipley published an article bearing severely upon one of Lola's friends, she armed herself with a riding crop and hunted for the object of her wrath.

She found him sitting in a saloon, and proceeded to give him a severe castigation but was disarmed. Both Lola and Shipley published their version of the affair, each one severely reflecting upon the character of the other.

From time to time Lola's old friends, the wealthy and elite, stopped by to see her, and she threw big parties with the champagne flowing freely. And she gave occasional performances for local crowds.

Still, in spite of these amusements, life in Grass Valley was scarcely as exciting for Lola as in Bavaria.

For a while she found diversion in promoting her protegé, a neighbor's child in whom she found stage talent. She taught her to sing and dance and toss her curls.

Little Lotta Crabtree was seven years old when she made her debut dancing an Irish jig on an anvil at a blacksmith. Whether Lola's training helped her or not, Lotta – vivacious and merry with red-gold hair and a carefree laugh – went on to become the toast of theater audiences for half a century.

But long before that happened, Lola had wearied of Grass Valley. And Grass Valley had wearied of Lola – the beautiful, the wayward. She packed up her velvet gowns, cleared out the champagne in the cellar, and left for Australia.

When the Australian performances went badly, she tried lecturing on women's rights in New York.

When that lulled audiences to sleep, she turned to religion, first as a spiritualist conversing with her historical counterparts – Madame Du Barry, Cleopatra and Mary Queen of Scots – and later as an Episcopalian.

By now she had exchanged her flamboyant wardrobe for shapeless gray wool frocks with high necklines and low hemlines.

But by summer 1860 she had even lost her zeal for evangelism.

At age 42 she was virtually without friends or funds.

When she died of a stroke that winter in New York only eleven mourners attended her funeral. The few dollars that remained of her fortune were willed to "the poor who are also poor in spirit."

In earlier, happier times, she had once remarked that historians would record her, Countess of Landsfeldt, as notorious, but would call Lotta famous.

It was an uncommonly accurate prediction.

Lotta Crabtree

Paragon of the gold rush theater was Lotta Crabtree, daughter of a luckless prospector and a boardinghouse mother in Grass Valley, a lusty mining town north of Sacramento.

Lotta was just six years old when the dazzling Lola Montez breezed into town and settled down with her pet bear two doors from the Crabtree home.

The bored and lonely entertainer was immediately drawn to the little girl with the red curls and began teaching her a few intricate dance steps and some simple ballads. She also taught her to ride horseback, and the pair could often be seen riding around the countryside, the six-year-old perched in front of the saddle.

Legend has it that Lotta's first performance was doing an Irish jig at Flippin's Blacksmith Shop in the nearby village of Rough & Ready, to the accompaniment of hammer on anvil and wild applause from the miners, most of whom were Irish.

But her big chance came a year later, after the Crabtrees had moved to Rabbit Creek. A local theater owner had seen Lotta's efforts and needed a child actress to meet competition from a rival who was featuring his small daughter with great success.

Her mother made for her a handsome Irish costume of green — long-tailed coat, knee breeches, tall hat. Her father made a pair of Irish brogues and whittled a shillelagh, and Lotta danced for the miners.

For the Irish miners, Lotta's vigorous Irish jig was deemed nothing short of sensational, and they showered the boards at her feet with nuggets and sacks of gold dust, even a gold slug worth fifty dollars.

Lotta Crabtree's career had begun.

A favorite with the miners was Little Lotta's performance as the Drummer Boy.

She and her mother toured the mining camps for years, often in grueling one-night stands. (Father was left behind to continue his profitless digging for gold.) She learned new songs and steps. A black minstrel taught her to do a soft-shoe breakdown. Jake Wallace taught her how to make a banjo ring. From others she picked up buck-and-wing and new bits of pantomine. Thus equipped, she could put on a whole show by herself.

With barrel-top numbers at auctions, variety billings in the mines and San Francisco, bits in the regular plays, and specialties between acts, Lotta had a busy childhood. In one little vibrant bundle of energy, she represented the things the Californians of this generation most prized: humor and pathos, high skill and lower buffoonery, mastery of the traditional forms, and indulgence in improvisation.

From the outset, Lotta was an uninhibited performer who endeared herself to audiences. As a teenager in the 1860s, she would appear on stage smoking a cigar — highly unladylike conduct for the times. But Lotta had a talent for simultaneously titillating miners and amusing matrons who would ordinarily be outraged by such behavior.

Later in her career, plays were written for Lotta, as well as adaptations of old standards. Audiences were enthralled by her portrayal of *Little Nell*.

Another favorite was *Jenny Leatherlungs*, a parody on the career of Jenny Lind, one of the most famous singers of the day.

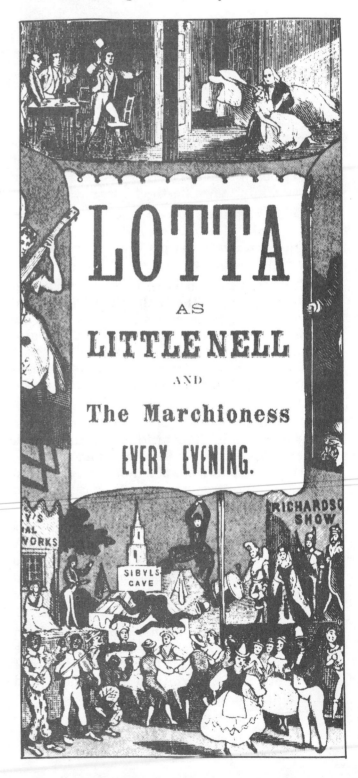

Undoubtedly the secret of Lotta Crabtree's vast success was her innocence. Whatever she lacked in dramatic ability, she made up for in personality. Where other actresses were tainted by scandal, Lotta was a lamb among wolves.

As she grew older, she introduced gaminlike bits into her acting – showing her knees by pulling up her stockings, rolling off divans with a flurry of lifted petticoats, and wearing the briefest of skirts. But it was all done with such guileless staging that even female spectators rarely objected.

She made her New York debut in June 1864 with only modest success. After three years of touring the country, however, she returned to New York in "Little Nell and the Marchioness," adapted for her from Dickens' "The Old Curiosity Shop," and was a sensation. From then until her retirement she enjoyed huge popularity at home and in England. Her infectious gaiety, perennially winsome, childlike appearance, and occasionally saucy and sweetly risque manner made her a versatile performer and ranked her in the forefront of the emerging theater scene of the West.

The 24-foot cast-iron monument at the intersection of Market and Kearney Streets in San Francisco was the gift of Lotta Crabtree to the city she loved, and which worshipped her. It has stood there for more than a hundred years. Its most memorable moment occurred in 1910 when opera singer Louisa Tetrazzini sang "The Last Rose of Summer" at its base. Thousands who had survived the earthquake mobbed the streets to hear her.

When Lotta retired at the age of forty-four she still had her red curls and flashing black eyes. She never married, though she had several prosperous lovers. And she never came out of retirement. Her mother had saved most of her daughter's enormous earnings – four million dollars which had its origins in the California gold fields, tossed by the hardened hands of miners upon the rough boards of frontier theaters.

It all went to charity.

Adah Menken

No comet ever blazed a more flaming path across the skies of the Early West than did Adah Isaacs Menken, who toured the region in the early 1860s, with particular success in the Nevada silver mining towns.

Adah was not a dancer like Lola nor a variety performer like Lotta. Her forte was melodrama. What made her so provocative was that she did what she did in a state of comparative undress. Moreover, she did it on a running horse — "a wild, untamed stallion of Tartary," the show bills called him.

Although she did appear in other melodramas, it was this performance in *Mazeppa* that was the most thrilling for audiences.

The story line of the play is taken from a Byron poem in which a Tartar prince is condemned, in the climactic scene, to ride forever in the desert stripped naked and lashed to a "fiery, untamed steed."

There was no way Adah could look like Prince Ivan, but trouper that she was, she didn't let that deter her.

Adah didn't exactly play the part of Ivan nude, but many thought she did. Newspaper accounts of the day differ in decribing her costume (it may have varied), but it was usually said to be either a short Greek tunic or tight-fitting underwear. Either way, her sparsely clad figure packed them in at boom-town theaters, prompting an overeager critic to state, "Prudery is obsolete now."

Not every reporter took his view, however. The illusion of nakedness caused another critic to write: "Her exhibitions are immodest, unfit for the public eye, degrading to women, whose sex is hereby depraved, and whose chastity is corrupted."

Menken began her western career in San Francisco at Maguire's Theater Saloon. But it was in Virginia City, Nevada that she was received with the greatest fanfare.

A *Mazeppa* poster still extant at Piper Opera House in that ghost town, shows Adah's languid form (apparently minus the tights) strapped to a wild, rearing stallion with rolling eyes. It is notable that the poster gives Adah top billing over famous writer J. Ross Browne, whose lecture following Adah was printed in much smaller type. The poster also contains ads for a couple of popular products of the day, Ayer's Tonic Pills and Brown's Bronchial Troches — together with a notice: Have a good meal at the Howling Wilderness Saloon!

How those silver miners loved Adah!

Virginia City was draped with posters for weeks before she arrived, and every miner in camp was worked up to fever pitch to see this gorgeous body in the flesh. When she got to her hotel, the volunteer firemen gatherred below her window to serenade her.

Mazeppa had a long run in Virginia City, and when it ended the miners showed their appreciation by presenting Adah with a gold bar worth $2,000, named a mine after her, and gave her fifty shares of that mine's stock — which she reportedly sold later for $50,000.

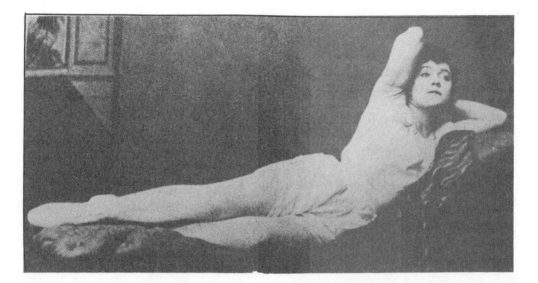

It wasn't only the miners. Reviewers liked her too. One of them was Mark Twain, reporter for the local *Territorial Enterprise*. Rising above his initial antipathy created by all the advance publicity, he gave her an unqualified rave after the performance.

In fact, he went to her hotel room afterwards to congratulate her. There he found her sipping champagne and feeding brandy-soaked tidbits to her kitten.

According to Twain's account, he read and appraised her poetry — she charmingly criticized his prose.

————————————

Adah Menken's personal life was every bit as volatile as her stage role in *Mazeppa*.

She was probably born in New Orleans in 1835, though facts concerning her early life are obscured by the confusing layers of publicity stories added later.

Adah was bright and became fluent in several languages — Hebrew, German, Spanish and French. She wrote passable poetry (she later published a book of verse and dedicated it to her friend Charles Dickens). She was an expert horsewoman (and claims to have ridden in the circus).

With all this activity, she still found time to marry at age 21 to Alexander Isaac Menken, whose name she retained through three more marriages and a number of infidelities.

Strikingly beautiful, she became the central figure in a scandalous divorce case in 1859. In the belief that Menken had divorced her, she married pugilist John Heenan. Menken then announced they were still married but proceeded to obtain a divorce, while Heenan denied their marriage.

Adah found little in common with Heenan, but apparently she got something of value out of the union, for at the height of her fame in Virginia City she startled the patrons of one saloon by offering to take on anyone in the room in a boxing match. The only man who responded was knocked down in the second round.

For twenty years Adah played her famous role and was strapped to a very real horse before fascinated western audiences. But on one day in 1864 during one of her performances, the horse had run too near "one of the flats" on stage and tore the flesh of Adah's leg. A Dr. Martin who was called to the theater during a rehearsal a week later stated that "a cancer growth formed."

It was her last performance. Adah Menken died at the age of 43.

The West's golden era for women of easy virtue was during the 1850s — a time when there was only one female for every 30 males.

Decent women were at a premium. One contemporary account relates that a widow in Sonora buried her husband one day and married the chief mourner the next afternoon. "If a woman is to stay pure in the licentious life of California," the journalist added, "her virtue must indeed be very firm."

Claim-happy prospectors were pouring into California, and they had nothing more than the memory of feminine companionship to warm them at night. The result was inevitable. Prostitution existed as a necessity, a social service, and a thriving industry in nearly every settlement in the West.

Unattached females, moved by the same spirit of adventure that attracted men to the West, arrived in the boomtowns in a dead heat with the first saloons.

Legend usually depicts these women as frolicsome harlots, splendid in lace and fancy goods, able to please for a dollar — or to love for nothing if the right man came along.

Indeed the legend was not without basis. "Lillie Lee would appear in a splendid Turkish costume," an observer reported, "which admirably displayed her tiny little foot encased in richly embroidered satin slippers."

The men, who had never seen the like, were captivated by these women, scarlet though they may have been. With them, the miners found elegance, companionship, sympathy, as well as a bed partner, and they often treated even the lowliest saloon girls with affection and respect.

Not all the women shared the good luck of Lillie Lee, of course. For many, it was simply an avenue to achieve economic independence in a time when domestic pay was less than $25 a month. As one Denver woman succinctly noted, "I went into the sporting life for business reasons and no other. It was a way for a woman in those days to make money, and I made it."

Some girls became the darlings of successful men. Jane Barnes, a barmaid who left England to travel to Oregon by ship in 1814, was the beloved of Donald McTavish, who had been sent to Oregon to govern a trading post of the North West Company. Jane's charms also enthralled the natives, and a Flathead Chinook offered her a life of ease; she need carry no wood or water, nor dig roots. Such a fate was spared her, but trouble loomed.

McTavish was drowned by a tidal wave. Adventurous Jane sailed for Cathay, and the last record of her was a bill to a London company from the ship's owners for her passage home.

As exciting as the lives of these scarlet women sometimes seemed, there were many who found a bitter end when their inventory reached a point of diminishing returns. Some died of malnutrition or quietly swallowed poison. Some endured years of privation, prayed and reformed, or did welfare work.

Extravagant or humble, charming or diamond-in-the-rough, they all formed a part of the rich fabric of the wild days of the Early West.

Julia Bulette

First came the miners who worked in the mines
Then came the ladies who lived on the line
                    ...Old Ballad

In Virginia City, the "line" was D Street.

And the queen of D Street, a legend of fabulous proportions in a city full of legends, was Julia Bulette.

Julia had a regal air about her; she was a beauty of considerable wit and charm, with remarkably good taste in every civilized aspect of life from vintage wines to canopied beds.

Her house was an oasis in a community of drab shacks and cheerless rooming houses, the only real homelike retreat the miners had, a well-appointed, well-regulated center of social life. She allowed no disorderly conduct; visitors had to behave at all times as gentlemen or out they went.

And to a man the miners adored her. "She may be scarlet," said one of them, "but her heart is pure white."

Later, when silver made the town rich, "Julia's Palace" became a cultural retreat where fine wines and the best in French cooking added to a delightful evening. She rode around town in a brougham with her own crest emblazoned on the door. At the theater she wore an opera hood of white silk and purple velvet and a sable scarf. Diamonds glittered at her throat.

One of Julia's friends was a man named Cunningham, a ranch owner in nearby Genoa. In addition to the ranch, he had a mine in Bodie from which he derived, from time to time, large sums of gold. Occasionally, when the gold piled up, he would drive a pair of fast geldings up the hill to Virginia City and throw parties for Julia which even in those days were fabulous. It was his pleasant custom to present Julia with a new diamond and the other lady guests with embroidered sacks of gold dust.

One year, on the Fourth of July, Cunningham came down to Virginia City and rented the

whole of one of the more luxurious C Street saloons and played host there to every lady then professionally active. The ladies could bring their own escorts or choose from the gentlemen present.

Entertainment was by stars of the opera house and such singers, dancers and trapeze artists as could be brought from San Francisco by special coach. A hundred gentlemen, and a like number of ladies, filled the establishment, partaking of such delicacies as green turtle soup, oysters brought from Puget Sound packed in ice, ragout of peacock breast, and souffle made with peaches that had been soaked in brandy. The banquet lasted until dawn.

To pay homage to the great Julia, the firemen made her an honorary member of Fire Engine Company No. 1. And on July 4, 1861 they elected her the Queen of the Independence Day parade. Crowned in a firemen's hat and carrying a brass fire trumpet filled with fresh roses, she rode Engine Company Number One's shiny new truck through the town, the red-shirted firemen marching behind. For the occasion she had designed a large banner which was mounted in front of the engine.

Julia took her membership in the fire company seriously, and donated money regularly for new equipment. Sometimes she brewed coffee and brought it to the men at the scene of the fire.

Julia gained fame not only for her voluptuous charms, but for her charitable acts. When an influenza epidemic hit the city, it was Julia who carried medicine and comfort from tent to shack to cabin.

And when the marauding Paiutes descended from the hills and threatened the populace, all the women were evacuated to Carson City. But brave Julia stayed behind to cheer the men on in battle.

But her wealth was her undoing. One dark night a Frenchman named Jean Millian knocked at her door When he departed he was carrying a trunk filled with Julia's furs and her jewels. And behind him he left Julia, strangled to death on her ornate canopied bed.

The town went into mourning. Saloons hung out black wreaths. The fire company covered its engines with black streamers. When the forces of law failed to turn up the murderer, there was talk of organizing a vigilante committee to track him down.

They gave Julia the finest funeral the Comstock ever saw. Thousands formed a procession of honor behind Julia's silver-handled casket — first the men of Fire Engine Company No. 1 in full-dress uniform, then the Nevada militia band playing the funeral dirge. A special glass-walled hearse carried Julia to the Flowery Cemetery east of town — but of course not in sanctified ground.

As the procession turned back toward town, the militia band broke into a sprightly rendition of "The Girl I Left Behind Me."

She was what she was, no doubt about that. And a night with Julia might cost up to a thousand dollars. But she had given the miners something above and beyond the chore of grubbing for silver. She had put charm into life.

When the murderer, Jean Millian, was apprehended almost a year later, the town felt little mercy. His hanging was one of the greatest outings Virginia City had known. The entire town turned out with picnic boxes and hundred-proof spirits.

Just before Jean Millian dropped through the trap door, he kindly thanked the ladies of the town for bringing him cupcakes during his incarceration.

That night, on C Street, drinks were on the house.

Madame Moustache

Eleanore Dumont, one of the more notorious of the West's "loose element," dealt both love and faro.

She was a pleasingly plump brunette in her mid-twenties, shy and modest, when she arrived in Nevada City, California in 1850 and started an elegant gambling saloon. On opening night free champagne in unlimited quantities was served to all customers, and her place was a smashing success.

Eleanore Dumont was at that time described as beautiful, dark-haired, and charmingly French. Every inch a lady, she allowed no profanity or ill behavior in her establishment.

She had a zest for games of chance and personally dealt at the faro tables. As she worked, she studied the moves of experienced gamblers, so that in time she herself became an excellent gambler.

"Poker Alice," one of the more notorious of gamblers in those rowdy days, called her "the best known woman gambler in the West," and added that Eleanore was clever, had charm, was a good musician and a linguist — "I never could understand why she became a gambler."

Poker Alice.

As the mines prospered, the rude mining camp of Nevada City turned into a tumultuous city with 79 saloons. The roaring life of miners who had struck gold brought prosperity to Eleanore.

But by 1859 Nevada City's gold was playing out, and the adventuresome, free-spending men who had once lined faro tables with their piles of chips packed up and left for brighter prospects — notably Virginia City, Nevada where the hills were found to be loaded with silver.

Eleanore shifted her operations from camp to camp, following the gold and silver strikes. When the Nevada mining boom collapsed, she drifted to Montana, New Mexico, and Colorado, picking up several lovers along the way. She spent some time running a parlor house in San Francisco, gave that up and set out for the hell-on-wheels towns that accompanied the Union Pacific's railroad construction across the continent, offering her services.

Her beauty faded, she drank too much. And when a shadow of down began growing on her upper lip, she was dubbed Madame Moustache by a disillusioned miner. She retained that sobriquet to the end of her life.

She knew how to defend herself with horsewhip or pistol if the situation demanded it. One night a couple of tough customers tried to hold her up on the way home with the house bank, demanding she give them her money.

She deftly reached into her skirt, but instead of money she brought out a small gun and plugged them. She killed one and the other escaped.

By 1877 Madame Moustache was running a brothel in Eureka, Nevada. She ended up in Bodie, where her luck ran out. She lost whatever little money she had left, playing in a faro game.

Discouraged, she finished her career by making herself a cocktail — half champagne and half prussic acid.

The Sacramento Union ran a brief dispatch from Bodie. "A woman named Eleanore Dumont was found dead today about a mile out of town, having committed suicide."

Little remains of Bodie, a town that wasn't much to begin with. Legend has it that a little girl in Truckee City, upon learning the family was moving there, prayed "Goodbye, God, I'm going to Bodie."

WOMEN VOTE FOR PRESIDENT

And for All Other Officers in All Elections on the Same Terms as Men in

Wyoming, Colorado, Utah and Idaho

The Women with a Cause

In spite of official reports from Congress and elsewhere that the country beyond the Mississippi River was a land of "cannibalism, wild beasts, deserts, mountains, and uncrossable rivers, pioneer women climbed into Conestoga wagons and headed west from the 1830s onward. Many of them made the frightening journey for altruistic reasons.

Eliza Spalding, a semi-invalid, left New York with her husband and another couple in 1836 and became one of the first white women to cross the Rockies. On the journey to Oregon she became even sicker from the buffalo meat the group ate regularly. She finally reached Oregon, where she taught religion, weaving and knitting to the Nez Perce tribes for many years.

Mary Atkins, an educated Midwestern woman, reached California in 1855 and became the head of' a Young Ladies' Seminary in Benicia. An educator, publicist and financial coordinator, she was compared by an admirer to a "sculptor chiseling the character of California

womanhood from primitive marble." In the mining world of the 1850s, she provided much needed education for women.

Biddie Mason, a slave who moved to California with her owner by ox cart in 1851, and won a legal battle to be freed, secured work as a midwife for $2.50 a week. She managed to save enough money to buy two city lots, which later became valuable and started her on her way to a fortune — much of which was used to turn her home into a refuge for stranded and needy black travelers.

Not all women of the West had to travel great distances to get there. The first women in the West were American Indian women. They were responsible, to a great extent, for the opening of the West to white settlers. Journals written by early pioneers tell how important Indian women were because of their knowledge and hardiness. They taught settlers how to live off the land, helped them establish relationships with western tribes, and often served as guides in unfamiliar territory.

Reported the *San Francisco Monitor* in August 1868: "The Pacific Mail steamer *Colorado* has brought a large addition to the Chinese population this week, destined according to Chinese custom, to slavery. But the vigilance of the police who took charge of them immediately on arrival and removed them to St. Mary's Hospital may succeed in spoiling the plans of their supposed masters."

Of the 35,000 Chinese living in the U.S. in 1860, only 1784 were women – and most of them were not "respectably married" women, they were slave girls or prostitutes, some as young as eleven or twelve, kidnapped in Hong Kong or Canton and spirited to West Coast cities to work in the brothels and sweatshops.

Brothels flourished unchecked throughout the 1850s and 1860s – a condition that missionary women were determined to change.

Into this lamentable scene came Donaldina Cameron, one of the most amazing women in San Francisco history. What she saw in Chinatown changed her life – and made of San Francisco a different place.

In the labyrinth of back alleys in old San Francisco Chinatown, little slave girls were kept behind barred doors. Easily forgotten bits of humanity they were, smuggled in like the opium their owners craved, bought and sold with the gold that was the currency in those historical days.

Ordinary domestic slaves sold for $100 to $500; the pretty creatures bartered to brothel keepers brought much larger sums.

Donaldina Cameron's Scots blood boiled. Joining forces with Maggie Culbertson at the Presbyterian women's Home Society, she set out to rescue the poor unfortunates from the vice dens – this at a time when anti-Chinese sentiment ran high and police frequently winked at what was going on.

Armed only with an umbrella and a police whistle, she set out to destroy the system. Off she went, down the back alleys of Chinatown and the secret underground passageways, breaking down doors, dropping through skylights, often literally yanking slave girls from the hands of their owners.

The owners called her *Fahn Quai* – the "she devil." Countless times she was marked for death. Effigies were hung, dynamite planted. It could not stop her.

In ways that were strange and devious, word would come to her of girls needing to be rescued. But it required courage for these messengers to come to the "she devil." A tong robbed of its valued slave was not to be taken lightly.

Foon Hing, who brought his cousin to the Home, found vengeance swift. No sooner was the grateful girl safely in the haven than a bullet laid him gasping on the sidewalk at the door.

With such tales rumored about, it was a terrified young Chinese man who came to the Home one Saturday and whispered his story. He had met a girl in a slave house who confided her troubles to him. Here she must earn enough to pay for all her food and clothing and clear $300 a month besides. She could stand it no longer.

He had tried to rescue her, but had been intercepted by a rival tong which was holding her and demanded a thousand dollars for her return. "Please you come quick," said the messenger. "No can get money. You come rescue her." Miss Cameron turned to her interpreter and said, "Come quickly, we must go on another rescue."

They picked up an Irish policeman at the corner — old and fat — and when they reached the tong hall he dealt with the Chinese door guard while Miss Cameron, all unprotected, flew down the hall, drawn by muffled screams. A huge oak door banged in her face.

The breathless policeman arrived on the scene, but he couldn't open the door either. He could get assistance, he thought.

The prettiest Chinese girls might achieve a higher standing as prostitutes — but they were never free from their life as "sing-song" girls.

Miss Cameron waited twenty minutes for him, frantically listening to the sounds of moving, smashing, banging, behind the impenetrable door, until at last three policemen came to batter it down. When no girl could be found the police prepared to leave in disgust. But Miss Cameron stepped out on a fire escape and a painter on a scaffold called to her, "They took her up through the skylight, across the roof next door."

Miss Cameron flew down a long flight of steep stairs, up another just as steep. The black-coated Chinese resident protested, "My daughter only girl here; fine Christian home."

It was puzzling. The skylight was open, but still no girl. Then Miss Cameron spotted a dresser out of line with the wall. At the magic words, "Mission Home" the trembling slave girl came out.

The conditions in which these slave girls lived were dreadful – or worse. Said one missionary from the Home, "They're fortunate if they have a hole in the roof to see daylight, or some dim old window, half-boarded up. One woman had never crossed the threshold since her arrival from China seven years before."

In the first thirteen years, the Home had two hundred admissions, secured eighteen letters of guardianship, and watched 55 marriages performed.

Over the years, Donaldina was credited with rescuing thousands of "sing-song" girls and bringing them back to the Mission, where they and their babies were cared for.

The girls called her *Lo Mo* – good mother. She taught them how to live again, educated them, found husbands for them. Some earned their passage and returned to China.

In time, the existence of Chinatown slavery became no more than a memory.

Donaldina Cameron lived to the age of 98.

Narcissa Whitman

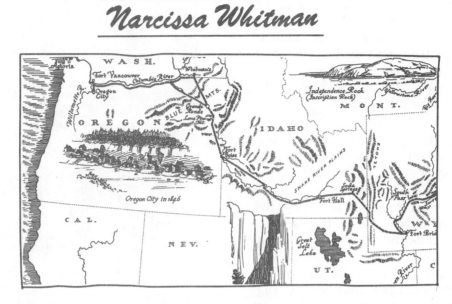

Not every woman who headed westward was in search of gold, love, or adventure. Narcissa Prentiss had a burning zeal to become a missionary and go west to convert the Indians.

She was described by her friends in glowing terms –"golden hair, symetrically formed, graceful in carriage, and possessed of sparkling eyes." But at 26 she was yet single (unusual for the times), and the church would not condone single women in the missionary service.

Her only hope lay in finding a husband with the same burning zeal.

By some extraordinary turn of fate, just such a young man appeared: Marcus Whitman.

The wedding ceremony was scarcely over before the Whitmans were ready to leave for Oregon for their evangelical tasks. The Reverend Perkins, an experienced missionary, expressed serious doubts about Narcissa's suitability for the rough life she faced. But the Whitmans believed zeal alone would carry them.

The journey itself enchanted Narcissa."Our manner of living is far preferable to any in the States," she wrote to her sister. "I never was so contented before."

The newlyweds arrived at Fort Vancouver and located a spot for the mission, among the Cayuse Indian tribe — not a very lucky choice. Unlike the more intelligent and devout Nez Perces, the Cayuses resented religion. "Some feel almost to blame us for telling them about eternal realities," wrote Narcissa.

But her uneasy thoughts were subordinated to something more important, the birth of a blond, blue-eyed girl.

Narcissa was lonely much of the time, for Marcus was off saving the souls of the Cayuse. They both were consumed with the sheer, never-ending drudgery of their work, and the Indians increasingly set up a resistant wall of laziness and abysmal ignorance, hardening slowly into active antipathy.

At the end of two years, to the joy of the Whitmans, nine new missionaries arrived to establish teaching centers among various tribes. However welcome, though, the added burden on Narcissa was beginning to show. Overburdened, the hard life and unbroken strain were showing up in frayed nerves.

Real tragedy struck when her child was found drowned. One of the servants reported he had seen two toys floating in the river. Marcus, intent on his Bible-reading, said only: "It is the Sabbath, let them be, we'll get them tomorrow." But Narcissa was terrified. She ran to the river and found her daughter caught in some roots at the bottom of the river.

After their daughter's death, eight difficult years were to pass before the horrendous disaster that ended the mission.

At times, Marcus was remarkably patient with the Indians. But in general, the Reverend Mr. Perkins had probably been astute in appraising the Whitmans as being too civilized, too proud, too aware of their own superiority. As he later told Narcissa's mother, "They did not 'identifiy' themselves with their Indian charges,"

In truth, the Cayuses were further than ever from a state of grace. Disturbed and agitated

Was it prophetic? Narcissa chose black bombazine for her wedding gown — the hue and material of formal mourning — and all her female relatives were dressed in black.

by the increasing number of white people, they were quite willing to listen to a couple of eastern half-breeds who were circulating among them saying what was probably true — their days as free men were numbered.

The measles epidemic was the fuse that lit the powder keg. Not only had Whitman failed to cure the sick, an ugly rumor was circulating that he was administering poison instead of medicine.

In July 1847, only four months before their murder by Indians they had come to Christianize, Marcus Whitman and his high-spirited wife Narcissa, entertained a wandering Canadian artist named Paul Kane who aspired to leave a record of Indian types. It was through this chance visit that a portrait has been preserved of the man who killed Marcus and incited fellow tribesmen to a heartless massacre of Narcissa and others in the lonely settlement at Waiilatpu, "the place of rye grass."

The 29th of November 1847 started as an ordinary day. The men were working as usual in the gristmill. Others were studying, sewing, cooking. Suddenly the Cayuses started shooting. Narcissa ran from another part of the mission to see what was happening, and was shot. Too weak to walk from loss of blood, she was carried from the house on a chair. Hardly had she appeared in the open than the shooting began again. The men carrying her were shot dead at once, and she was struck by a number of bullets. An Indian rushed up and thrust her face down into the thick November mud while another Indian lifted her head by its long hair and struck her face viciously. No one knows how long it took her to die.

For her, however, death came sooner than for Marcus. Some of the terrified occupants of the mission house, still in hiding, heard his groans far into the night.

Having satisfied their thirst for revenge, the Cayuse withdrew to their own lodges. They returned the next day, though, to feast on mission stores.

The anxious settlers in lower Oregon, learning of the massacre, were quick to pursue the murderers. The Cayuse. now running the mission for their own use, fled into the hills at the approach of the riflemen. But after two years of desperate wandering, five of them voluntarily gave themselves up. When asked why he had surrendered, one of them answered, "Did not your missionaries teach us that Christ died to save his people? So we die to save our people."

Detail on this 1847 sketch of the massacre is incorrect. Narcissa was actually in another part of the mission when the Indians arrived.

Sarah Winnemucca

Luckily for the first white trappers who ventured into the Great Nevada Basin, the Paiute tribe had preserved a myth that the world had begun with two couples, one white the other dark. After a quarrel the white couple vanished — but one day, promised the myth, they would return.

Thus when Chief Truckee saw strange, pale men approaching, he joyfully welcomed them.

For his granddaughter, Sarah Winnemucca, his fondness for the white man was the most formative influence in her life. Growing up, she attended a white school, adopted white clothes and customs, even became a translator for the United States Army.

Still, her heart was always with her people; she never lived long apart from her tribe. If they suffered, she suffered. When they went hungry, she did also.

Sadly, her naive belief in the goodness of the white man was to be dashed.

Silver was discovered in Nevada and her homeland was overrun by the pale strangers — mining the land the Paiutes considered theirs. When the territory was elevated to statehood, the Paiutes were relegated to grim camps on the fringe of the silver fields.

Before long the Indians had become angry and rebellious. And Sarah's father, Chief Winnemucca — an inept leader — had neither the power to control his people or to negotiate with the white "intruders."

It was 20-year-old Sarah who stepped in, exhorted the Paiutes to behave themselves, and set out to appeal to the newly appointed Nevada Governor to help smooth relations between Indians and whites. She also made a long trip on horseback to the San Francisco Presidio to call on the General of the U. S. Army for help.

But the General was indifferent ("not my responsibility") and the Governor quickly forgot commitments he had made.

Meanwhile, things were going badly back on the reservation. The agent appointed by the Indian Bureau, whose duty it was to look out for the interests of the Paiutes, was exploiting them instead — selling reservation timber, leasing grazing rights to white cattlemen, operating a retail store with provisions shipped by the government for the Indians. When he started stocking gunpowder, forbidden for Indian use, Sarah told him he was asking for trouble.

The agent thought her impertinent, and before long Sarah was called upstate to Fort McDermitt to answer charges of Paiute insubordination to the Indian Bureau agent.

Sarah sat poised before her adversaries and gave an impassioned account of the abuses which provoked the problem. Before she was through, she had turned the issue around — from a white grievance to an Indian grievance.

Sarah negotiated an agreement that allowed the Paiutes to leave the reservation and their gouging agent, and to occupy a campsite on the fringe of the military base.

This skirmish was the first of many similar that Sarah met and settled in the years that followed. The principals in each scenario had different names, but the story was always the same – officials who made promises they didn't keep, Indian Bureau agents who took advantage of those they were sent to help, and problems with her own people who so quickly lost faith in her when things went wrong.

Occasionally things went very right. One agent taught the Paiutes how to farm their land and store food for the winter, even gave permission for them to go hunting and have feasts in their traditional way.

That didn't last. The good agent was replaced by another demon.

The worst that happened, though, was when the Bannock tribe went on the warpath, taking many Paiutes prisoner.

Learning of the uprising, the Army appointed Sarah a scout and sent her to find their encampment and persuade the Bannocks to give up their war.

Sarah rode her horse for two days at break-neck speed, non-stop, until she made it to the Bannock camp. To avoid detection, she stole unnoticed into camp wearing paint and blanket. She found her father there and explained that the Army was en route to attack the Bannocks, and that the captives must flee in order not to be part of the attack.

The rugged mountain where Paiutes were held captive.

That night her father and the remaining Paiutes left the camp under cover of darkness, followed in close pursuit by the Bannocks. Sarah realized that the only hope was for her people to hide while she rode ahead to the troops for help.

"That was the hardest work I ever did for the government in all my life," she later wrote. "The whole round trip, from morning June 13 to June 16, arriving back at 6:30 p.m., having been in the saddle night and day, distance, about 223 miles...I, only an Indian woman, went and saved my father and his people."

But her efforts were not over. She was asked to return with the Army as interpreter/guide to vanquish the Bannocks.

The Bannocks led the Army on a grueling six-week chase up rugged peaks, through plunging canyons, over hot alkaline desert. Sarah, who knew the territory better than any soldier, galloped about carrying dispatches between Army units. At night she read Indian signal fires. During the final battle that routed the Bannocks so they never rallied again, Sarah was the bravest of scouts, moving constantly about the front lines.

For her bravery and loyalty, Sarah might have expected a largesse of gratitude. Instead, she was cruelly duped again.

The outcome for her tribe was not favorable. Although the Paiutes were innocent of any insurrection, the Army's General Howard, peevish because he had not favored the conflict in the first place, retaliated by sending the bedraggled, half-starved refugees first to Camp Harney in Oregon – then informing them they must march, in the dead of winter, to a prisoner camp in Yakima, Washington Territory.

Sarah's strident protests created not a ripple in the official plans. And her own people accused her of selling them out.

What could she do now? She brought her cause to the attention of people in San Francisco, lecturing everywhere. Declaiming dramatically on the duplicity of the Indian Bureau, Princess Winnemucca became the sensation of San Francisco.

Reports of Sarah's bold indictments so alarmed WashingtonD.C. officials that they invited her and her family to come for a visit, all expenses paid.

To her surprise, the Secretary of the Interior gave her everything she asked for – if she just wouldn't make speeches in Washington.

She was taken to the White House where President Hayes signed an executive order permitting the Paiutes to leave Yakima, and allocating to every adult male 160 acres of land. Each family would receive enough canvas for a tent. They even gave Chief Winnemucca a new suit of clothes.

It was a brilliant victory. But one by one, as she sought to collect on the promises, she learned they were worthless. The camp director at Yakima refused to recognize the paper since it had not been directored to him. All they really got was a nice trip and a new suit of clothes.

Sarah wouldn't give up. She was off to Boston, where she delivered a series of lectures under the auspices of the most aristocratic members of society. Her gripping accounts of the Paiute's misfortunes gave her audiences ample scope for indignation. Speaking engagements poured in from New York, Connecticut and Pennsylvania.

With the help and sponsorship of Mrs. Horace Mann, she wrote an autobiographical book about the Paiutes' troubles.

She appeared before a Congressional committee and spoke for a bill that would allow the Paiutes to be settled on land of theirown. It passed.

But even that victory melted away. The Secretary of the Interior refused to implement the legislation, and a new Congress did not force the issue.

Deeply depressed, she retired to Lovelock, Nevada and idled away her days. Not until the 20th century did the harshness of the Indian policy soften.

Still, Sarah Winnemucca's many daring feats put her into the ranks of American Indian heroines, alongside Pocohontas and Sacajawea.

Sarah, in the deerskin dress in which she spoke to the people of Boston.

The Outlaws

The Early West attracted a legion of nonconforming women: mavericks, loners, eccentrics, adventurers — and a few who fell into the dangerous and usually unprofitable career of the outlaw.

These female desperados were out to prove they were as capable as any man of swindling greenhorns, stealing cattle, holding up banks, and shooting with deadly accuracy.

Their exploits made news from coast to coast, adding an odd aura of adventure — even glamour — to the "Wild West" experience.

Some became legends in their own time.

Pearl Hart, locked up in an Arizona jail (the only female there), was surprised to receive an elderly woman visitor one day. She said she wanted to see the "famous bandit" and get an autograph for her young niece.

A STARR HAS SET.

Sudden Death of Cole Younger's Former Wife in the Choctaw Nation.

Special to the Globe.

FORT SMITH, Ark., Feb. 5.—Belle Starr, the former wife of Cole Younger, now serving a life sentence in the Stillwater penitentiary for bank robbery and murder at Northfield, Minn., died in the Choctaw Nation yesterday. The death of this notorious woman closes a remarkable and very interesting career, probably not equaled in romance by that of any other woman. Her whole life has been spent with desperate and lawless classes of men, and her own prowess as a crack shot and desperate woman has been, for some years, the talk of the entire Southwest, where most of her life has been spent. Rumor connects her with the famous James and Younger gangs in Missouri, and with various latter day notorieties. For some years she had lived in the "Nation" and had been in Fort Smith on business and as a witness in the United States court. After the imprisonment of her husband, Cole Younger, she married Samuel Starr, and lived with him in the Choctaw nation. With her husband she was in Fort Smith about three years ago, and the two left for home in the evening, but on the way Starr was killed. They stopped at a dance across the river, where they met an old enemy named West. Starr pulled his pistol and shot West through the groin, but when in the death throes West managed to pull a pistol and shot Starr, both dying about the same time. Belle was in another room at the time, and upon hearing of the shooting, took two pistols, one in each hand, and went out to do her share of the killing. But when she arrived both men were dead. Soon afterward she married her late husband's cousin, James Starr, a tall, well formed Indian, with long hair falling over his shoulders. He was in town yesterday when the telegram announcing her death was received. There was bad blood in his eye when he heard the news, and without delay he saddled his horse, provided himself with a quart of whisky and struck out on the run for home, saying somebody was going to suffer. Belle Starr figured in the United States court in this city on several occasions, and was once sent to the penitentiary for selling whisky in the "nation." Dressed in men's clothes, mounted on a spirited horse, and armed with a brace of formidable pistols, she raided, caroused and participated in every form of outlawry prevalent in the nation. She rode with grace, shot with great skill, and with it all was a well educated and accomplished woman. Many citizens of Fort Smith have heard her play on the piano in this city. She leaves one daughter named Pearl Younger, a beautiful girl, possessing the mother's fire and father's reckless criminalities.

Calamity Jane Canary, a boozy and disreputable hanger-on in saloons from Cheyenne southward, was the consort of teamsters, bullwhackers, and other hardened persons of the staging stations and Army posts. She wore men's clothing and swore men's oaths. She claimed to have been a Pony Express rider, and also the wife of Wild Bill Hickok, near whom she was eventually buried.

The record showed her to be something of a rough diamond in aiding the needy and destitute. At one time she faced the footlights, shooting out property mirrors; but her intemperate way of life caused her to miss lines and ad lib with bullwhacker's language, so she soon lost the one legitimate employment of her life.

Rose of Cimarron, one of the more mysterious women outlaws, is said to have become an outlaw in order to be with her sweetheart, George (Bitter Creek) Newcombe. One of the controversial incidents in her outlaw career was the gunfight at Ingalls, Oklahoma, during which she is said to have crossed a street full of flying lead, a rifle concealed beneath her flowing skirts to give her lover so he could escape. Rose later married a homesteader and settled down to raise a family.

Cattle Annie and Little Britches peddled whiskey to Indians, stole horses, rustled cattle, and occasionally robbed a bank. After considerable gunfire and face-scratching, they were at last taken custody and shipped to a reform school. Little Britches later turned to religion, died in a New York slum. Cattle Annie returned to Oklahoma to take up respectability.

✳━━━━━━━━━━━━━━━━━━━━━━━━━━━━━━━✳

Etta Place began her outlaw career when she fell in love with Harry Longbaugh, "The Sundance Kid." She wore a revolver and men's clothes. After their first holdup netted only $400 she decided to assume future planning for the gang. The trio found good success in the holdup business and teamed up with Butch Cassidy after he ingeniously gassed bank clerks with a skunk his horse had accidentally killed. Etta went with Sundance and Butch to Argentina, but was spared their miserable fate when they were trapped in a canyon and gunned down. She suffered an attack of appendicitis and had to be taken to Denver.

Belle with her lover, Blue Duck.

Belle Starr was the well-adjusted daughter of upper-class parents who settled in Texas. After the Civil War, Belle met and was seduced by Cole Younger, who rode with Frank and Jesse James, and she turned to a life of crime, exchanging one male partner for another through a long line of husbands and paramours, all outlaws. Only once did she get convicted, though she was involved in enough holdups to fill a large catalog. Her blazing career was stopped by a bullet in the back one day in 1889.

Pearl Hart, an Arizona girl of limited mentality, teamed up with Joe Boot, an ineffectual mining prospector, to rob an Arizona stagecoach. It was not entirely successful. After picking up $400 by robbing the passengers, they trotted their horses down the main road, then hoping to confuse pursuing officers, got lost themselves in a canyon. For their efforts Pearl got five years (Joe got twenty). On the whole, though, the caper didn't turn out too badly. Pearl was paroled after two years and made a stage tour billed as "the Arizona Bandit."

Queen of the Stolen Horses